Café Capriccio's Chef's Table

Front cover photo:
Jeanette Stanziano's family in the mid nineteen thirties, happily gathered around
a holiday table in the Bronx, New York. To me it is a magnificent evocation of the
sacred "Sempre famiglia" concept to which this book is also dedicated. JR

Back cover photo:
Photo by Jeanette Stanziano, whose presence is found from back to front. JR

Café Capriccio's Chef's Table
Copyright © 2012 by Jim Rua

Illustrations by Elisabeth L. Vines
Book design by Rita Petithory

Printed in the United States of America

The Troy Book Makers • Troy, New York • thetroybookmakers.com

To order additional copies of this title, contact your favorite local bookstore
or visit www.tbmbooks.com

ISBN: 978-1-935534-xxx

Café Capriccio's Chef's Table

SEMPRE FAMIGLIA

ORIGINAL RECIPES & COOKING TECHNIQUES
FAMILY RECOLLECTIONS
A FEW MEMORABLE CHARACTERS

JIM RUA

FABULOUS SPECIAL-OCCASION COOKING
FOR FAMILY AND FRIENDS

Contents

Jeanette Stanziano:

You inspired me to write this book.
I hope you can be proud of it.

With Love, JR

Dedication

THIS BOOK IS FOR YOU

All Tests Completed, Trials Endured, Faith Affirmed
You are Now our Leader.
As You are Mine, I Smile and Wonder
Who Will Your Successor Be?

Special thanks to Byron Nilsson
who read through all of my extemporaneous recipe notations,
rendering them legible and, to tell the truth,
improving them, again, and again.
Grazie infinite, amico mio.

We may live without poetry, music and art;
We may live without conscience and live without heart;
We may live without friends;
We may live without books;
But civilized man cannot live without cooks.
He may live without hope, – what is hope but deceiving?
He may live without love, – what is passion but pining?
But where is the man that can live without dining?

Source: Lord Lytton, from Luczzile (pt. 1, canto II)

Background and Brief History

This is the third book in a series about a lifetime of work in Albany, New York, at a small restaurant named Café Capriccio. I started this restaurant in 1982 and ten years later wrote a book about it called *Café Capriccio, A Culinary Memoir.* The book is about the life and vicissitudes of a restaurant and its people over a ten-year-span. It also includes recipes for the Café's signature food preparations which were developed during the period of ten years.

Many patrons and others enjoyed the book and so I wrote another one a few years later named *The Pasta Lovers Fast Food Cookbook, A Modern Approach to the Mediterranean Diet.* In the second book I provided simple recipes for pasta dishes that could be prepared quickly and inexpensively—but in accordance with good cooking practice, the way we make sauces and cook pasta dishes at Café Capriccio. My goals were to give new meaning to the concept "fast food," to expand the repertory of busy and sometimes budget-minded pasta lovers, to extol the virtues of modern supermarkets, and to describe a cuisine as delicious as it is healthful.

The third book in this series, the one you are reading, is about Café Capriccio's Chef's Table, a small, elegant dining room and kitchen where I have been cooking special dinners for groups of ten to sixteen guests for more than ten years. Dinner at the Chef's Table consists of five or more antipasti served family style, followed by a course of pasta or risotto, followed by a main course with *contorni* (selections of vegetables, potatoes, polenta, rice, cous cous, as appropriate) and finished with dessert. Chef's Table dinners also feature abundant wine selections that vary with the menus.

From a personal culinary perspective, there are two particularly interesting aspects of functions at the Chef's Table. The first is that most people who reserve the Chef's Table for their special occasions allow me to indulge my own food fancies with their menus. Consequently, I have been able to experiment with an extensive array of preparations, most based on frequent travels in Italy, Spain, and Portugal (as well as, I must say, the West Coast of the United States) during the past three decades. This degree of culinary freedom is significant, because restaurant cooks, no matter how creative, must function within a far more narrow range than other cooks. Menus in restaurants cannot change too frequently. Daily specials do provide creative opportunities, but specials also exist within fairly strict limits, often governed by financial or availability concerns. In contrast, the cooking we do at the Chef's Table is almost completely unrestrained.

The second aspect, which is really a discovery and the basis for this book, is that the foods we love best to cook and enjoy together are those we prepare family style, arrange on beautiful platters and in bowls, and then pass around to start our meal. The discovery is that this kind of family style preparation and dining (communal dining if you prefer) can accommodate the entire range of Italian regional cuisine (in fact any cuisine or mix of cuisines) and is an excellent approach for home cooks who love to entertain friends and families on special occasions around their own "chef's table."

Dinner at the Chef's Table begins with five or more dishes that we call "antipasti" prepared and served family style on beautiful platters or in bowls. If the table includes a dozen or more guests I will prepare as many as eight "antipasti." Guests pass around the platters, helping themselves to whatever they fancy. Cooking this way, I soon realized that this part of our meal, usually intended to awaken the appetite for courses to follow, is instead the most varied, interesting, and satisfying aspect of our dining experience – for the cooks and diners alike.

The foods we prepare and present "family style" for this course actually represent the entire range of Italian cuisine. At the Chef's Table, we follow this abundant and convivial presentation with pasta (first course for the

Italians), a main course (called second course in Italian), and then dessert. No matter how good the courses that follow, however, our guests are usually happiest with – and the cooks proudest of – the bountiful feast that begins every dinner at Café Capriccio's Chef's Table.

This book is about preparing and presenting our favorite Chef's Table dishes in the "family style." We will not use the terms "antipasto," "first course," or "second course" because these bountiful and beautiful preparations constitute the meal itself. In your hands, when you entertain family and friends, your chef's table will be as varied, colorful, bountiful and beautiful as you choose to make it. It can include all the foods you love to make: vegetables, salads, fish, shellfish, pasta, grains, polenta, meats… cooked in all the ways you love to cook: grilling, roasting, steaming, baking…. Our recipes will thus be organized around cooking methods, rather than courses. Sections will include headings such as Grill It, Roast It, Steam It, Stuff It, Skewer It, and Braise It.

This book is intended to assist you with techniques and choices when cooking for family and friends. It is especially suited for any occasion that calls for intimate gatherings around your chef's table where glorious food can be prepared, set down to be admired, and then passed around for everyone's enjoyment – not least the cook's, whose work should be finished when the bell rings for dinner.

The recipes provided in this book suppose that the cook will be preparing many dishes to serve guests. Consequently, indicated portions presume that each guest will select small portions of several choices. Recipes are always intended as guidance, and they forever beg to be improved by you and me and all others who enjoy cooking. The recipes do not therefore specify amounts of salt and pepper, garlic, lettuce, and herbs needed; these decisions are left to the individual culinary personality of the cook.

Additionally, these recipes are designed for eight to ten dinner guests. Quantities should be adjusted proportionally if you have more or fewer guests at your table.

Rua Family Table

The author demanding dinner from his parents at an early age

I grew up at a time when the daily routine for some families included dinner together. Mine was such a family. My family consisted of mom and dad; sisters Helene, Marlene, and Andrea; and me, the first child and only son. We lived in Kingston, NY, from the time I was about three years old until I went off to college at eighteen, in 1961.

Everybody loves his mother's cooking, especially when recalling it after she is no longer available to prepare her specialties. Holiday meals, birthdays, and the routine Sunday family meals we used to share now seem so special in our memories; we never thought they would end. My mother cooked all the foods we loved but cooking was not her passion; she didn't eat so much, either. Mom was a life-long member of the one-hundred-pound club—not for any effort on her part, just because that's the way it was for her.

My sisters and I were always clamoring for pasta, so our mother made us wonderful macaroni dishes, almost always with "meat sauce" simmered together with tomatoes and the holy-staple-ingredients of olive oil, garlic, basil, salt and pepper. Nothing else was needed, except a big salad to conclude the meal. Salad always finished our meals, followed by a small sweet treat enjoyed by my father with his post prandial coffee. My father said that salad made you feel lighter after consuming a big meal, and it assisted with the digestive process.

The preferred salad greens at the Rua family table were chicory (which we called endive) and escarole, two mildly bitter lettuce varieties that I still crave. As a kid, I never ate dessert because I loved so much the fresh salads prepared by my mother or father, tossed simply with olive oil, vinegar, salt, and pepper. For me, something sweet to conclude a good meal at my parents' table spoiled the taste and memory of the salad and of all that preceded it – except on my birthday, of course, when mom made me a special dinner, with a birthday dessert.

The birthday dinner ritual for me growing up consisted of my mother's stuffed rigatoni, a big salad, and then my birthday "cake," a delicious cheesecake with graham cracker crust. I can still taste it. The stuffed rigatoni recipe is included in this book, but I never learned the secret of my mom's graham cracker cheesecake.

My parents were devoted collaborators with well defined roles. Mother was mother and father was father. Father's overriding responsibilities during the period of this recollection (the decade of the 1950s) were first to be the provider; and second, to know what was best for his family, not least important regarding what was best for the family table. My father loved to cook, and my mother was his biggest fan and best collaborator. She knew that cooking was dad's passion, and I have to say as a close observer that mom always seemed to nourish dad's passions, so well did they understand each other. When dad wanted to cook, mom happily stepped aside.

The story of my father's culinary specialties begins with the principle of simplicity: cold-morning breakfasts on Saturdays and sometimes on Sunday after church. The breakfast would include sliced potatoes with onions and peppers fried crisp in a cast iron skillet, with bacon fat as the primary agent of my father's specialization. The potatoes were deeply colored and were served with eggs, sunny side up. I was always hungry in those days, which I believe prompted my father to "provide" a championship breakfast for a growing and active boy when most Italian Americans (and Italians) eschewed the morning meal opting for strong coffee (or cappuccino) and a sweet roll. My sisters loved these breakfasts as much as I did, but I never remember my mother eating anything. She always made the coffee, though, which was her specialty. The pot she used was the old percolator variety, made of flimsy aluminum, which nevertheless produced coffee good enough to bring a smile to the face of this life-long coffee lover.

My father frequently made the "sauce" for our family's pasta, one of his favorite contributions to our family table. Our family often added substantial cuts of meat to the tomato sauce: pork spare ribs, short ribs of beef, pork chops, sausage and of course *polpetti*, meatballs. The kids were always allowed to dunk crusty bread into the sauce as it was bubbling. I insist even now that the best way to taste the long cooking sauces is to dip a heel of bread into the sauce after it has cooked for an hour or so. At the Rua family table, pasta tossed with tasty meat sauces would be served separate but along with the meat that would constitute the main event at the table. Meat sauces like these, I must add, were usually prepared for Sunday dinner, and we did not eat so elaborately during the week.

My father possessed one particular culinary gift superior to all others: his virtuosity at the charcoal grill. This grill was the simplest of cooking devices, purchased for a few dollars at the local hardware store. On his grill, my dad prepared the most delicious steak, chicken, and sausage. This is what he grilled: steak, chicken, and sausage; his family could never get enough of it.

Grilling was done either just outside the garage door, a few steps from the kitchen, or, during inclement weather, one step into the garage, with the "overhead door" wide open to prevent asphyxiation. My father's grilling was never impeded by weather. The steak I loved most was sirloin with a round or elongated bone in the middle (a cut of meat I don't see any more in super markets), seasoned with salt and pepper and grilled over *carbon* (charcoal). The chicken was similarly seasoned and grilled the same way. The sausage often came to us from my cousin Michael Tiano whose family raised a couple of pigs every year, butchered them, and made mountains of sausage for the entire family. Nothing fancy–never any fancy cooking from my father–but in the hands of a grilling virtuoso like him the results were sublime.

My father's refined and simple culinary inspirations seem certainly to have derived from his parents. So much of their life revolved around the table, its rituals, and the sources of its bounty. Nevertheless, my grandparents' relationship to food was very different from that of my immediate family, and it was anything but simple. If the principle of simplicity governed my parents' table, the principle of self sufficiency governed the table of my grandparents.

My grandparents, Pietro and Giuseppa La Rocca Rua, lived in East Kingston, a small community of immigrants on the Hudson River. They came to America around the turn of the century – 1899 for my grandfather and shortly thereafter for my grandmother. She was born in Sicily (December 5, 1892); he was from Cosenza, Calabra (July 3, 1883). They met and married in the U.S., enjoyed long lives, and had at least twelve children.

My grandfather worked "on the brick yard," as they used to call it, making bricks. The brick yards on the Hudson around Kingston, NY, were major employers of the men in East Kingston during the period of my father's early life, certainly from 1915 when he was born until the beginning of World War II. Life was difficult, but the residents of East Kingston were extremely resourceful and above all self reliant.

My grandparents' food self sufficiency impressed me as a child and still inspires me today. I remember an enormous garden with fruits and vegetables. Berries of all kinds, grape vines, and fruit trees were abundant. My grandmother was a fabulous baker and there were always pies and pastries in her kitchen made from the fruit of trees, bushes, and vines in the back yard. Honey-coated deep-fried dough with powdered sugar, cookies, and small Sicilian-style pick up desserts were always temptingly available in my grandmother's kitchen. I also recall sharp provolone cheese, small trays of olives, and dark round loaves of bread that were always laid out for anyone passing through the house.

I remember myself as a small child, four or five years old, cuddled behind grandma's wood fired stove in a small space created by the exhaust vent that separated the stove from the wall. This was the place to be for a twenty-five pounder on a cold day in winter. The oven for this stove, full of good things and tantalizing aromas, was an extra compartment on the top of the stove that captured heat and was used as an oven.

My grandparents' vegetable garden was imposing and sustained the large family not only in summer but also throughout the rest of the year. Late summer harvest was a time when all the women in the family (and a few men and a few kids, including me) gathered for the "canning process," which was devoted to preserving fruits and vegetables until the next harvest. Everything that could be canned was canned. I especially remember the vegetable salads, vinegar peppers, and bright green beans that somehow retained their crisp texture and summer taste when we opened the jars months later when snow was on the ground. Grandma's cellar contained hundreds of "bell jars" with preserved fruits and vegetables that my family enjoyed all the year. Canned tomatoes especially were delicious in winter, during an era when decent tomatoes could be purchased for only a brief period after the first harvest in July. My family used to make a delicious salad with a jar of Grandma's tomatoes, flavored with basil, to which my mother or father would add thin sliced sweet onion, slivered garlic, olive oil, salt, and pepper – growing up, that salad was to me a desert island staple – and it still is.

Chickens roamed around my grandparents' house, hunting and pecking for food. I can only now recall, after more than a half century of repression, the first time I saw my grandmother take a chicken by its neck and whack its head off. I was shaken as the chicken ran around for a while before falling still. I never got used to this, nor did I relish the cleaning of fish and small game, the scent of which kept me out of my grandparents' basement from about the age of reason.

Most men in my family were hunters and fishers as were the male members of every other East Kingston family. They hunted rabbits, squirrels, and some birds for many months of the year. Big game could always be seen in the autumn hanging from one tree or another to "season." Not only deer were seasoned outside; I remember encountering on a fine late autumn day when I was about ten an enormous black bear eviscerated and swinging in the cool air next to grandma's house.

I will never forget one particular pasta dish my grandmother served to a crowd at her table when I was in the first or second grade. The sauce was made with squirrel, and the kids were told to be careful not to swallow the buckshot that came from the gun of the hunter, one of my uncles. My portion was full of buckshot and I thought it was as good as it gets at the table, but I confess never being tempted to take up the gun or the fishing rod, either for sport or self sufficiency.

Living near the Hudson River also provided the family with a major resource for fish, even in the winter when we fished through the ice. My father told me many times that people used to drive cars on the Hudson in January and February. There was no sign of global warming when my dad was a boy. Fishing through the ice on the Hudson River in the bitter cold of winter was not a sport but rather one more means for the resourceful immigrant families in East Kingston to sustain themselves and enrich the family table. There was always an abundance of fresh fish (including eels) from the river, usually fried, on my grandparents' dinner table.

Some families in East Kingston, including my Tiano cousins, raised pigs and made sausage for everybody in the community. My dear cousin Mike Tiano told me not long ago that in the old days whenever you fried a pork chop at home everybody in the neighborhood could smell it. Everybody knew what you were cooking, unlike today when pork is bred to be lean and tasteless. Nothing was lean and tasteless at dinner time in East Kingston when I was a boy.

We often traveled the short distance to my grandparents' house for the traditional late afternoon Sunday dinner. There would always be a crowd, representatives from my grandparents' brood of many children, their spouses, my cousins — but rarely guests from outside the family. The Tiano family mentioned above included my father's oldest sister, Aunt Rose Tiano, who lived next door to my grandparents (her parents) with her husband, Uncle Mickey Tiano, and four sons. Next to her lived her youngest brother, my uncle Frank Rua with his wife, Aunt Nina Tiano. There are two unrelated Tiano families in this story; Aunt Nina was not related to Uncle Mickey. However, to give the reader an idea of how tight these families were, and something of the flavor of East Kingston, I recall that at about six years old when I hung around my grandparents' house, the next door neighbor was Mr. Charles ("Blue") Tiano and his wife Jenny (parents of Aunt Nina). Next to them lived Uncle Frank and Aunt Nina, recently wed. And next to them lived Uncle Mickey Tiano and Aunt Rose Rua Tiano with their children. I do not mean this to be a lesson in genealogy but only an indication of the way life was lived in that town so long ago and yet so fresh in my memory.

During the 1950s several of my father's siblings lived in the New York area and would visit regularly, but not often. Their appearances were therefore especially exciting and festive. Grandma's Sunday "chef's table" was full to

overflowing with abundant food and a crowd of dinners whose common blood lines, hair patterns, skin colors, the shape of noses, manners of expression would be apparent to anyone who happened upon the occasion. Not that everyone looked alike, but this was a family – no doubt about it.

Sunday dinner at Grandma's would not be a hurried event. Dinner with fifteen or twenty family members of all ages is a sociological phenomenon involving a broad range of human experience: cooks had to cook for a crowd; women served the table and took care of the dishes; children had to be corralled, chased, loved, admired and cajoled; adults had their own things to talk about: brothers, sisters, in-laws.

Of course Grandma was the mother of all cooks. Her daughters Teresa, Josie, Marie, and Rose (who died before I was a teenager) cooked just like their mother. Never was there a shortage of culinary talent on Sundays at Grandma's table. The menu would usually include roasts of chicken, pork or game, salads and vegetables, abundant pasta, and plenty of sweets. The bread served in those days often came from a local woman who made crusty and dark ten-pound loaves in a wood oven. This bread, truly the staff of life, was delivered to our house once a week by my cousin Mike Tiano, called "Junie" by the family. Junie has always been devoted to family causes and continues to provides us with his marvelous vegetables, sausage that he still occasionally makes, and fresh fish from the pristine Ashokan Reservoir where he fishes every morning at about four in the morning during the season.

I grew up around good cooking and good cooks. And I learned to cook myself during almost thirty-five years of work in the kitchens of my own restaurants in addition to travel around the world paying attention to food. When I think about the most important antecedents and inspirations for my work at Café Capriccio, I realize they derive from the security, intimacy, and simple abundance I experienced at the tables of my parents and grandparents. One of the most satisfying experiences for me now is to entertain families on special occasions at the Chef's Table, just as my grandmother did for her family at her table. If my staff and I are able to bring to a large group celebrating a family event some part of the joyful legacy from my own family, I know the meal will be a satisfying experience for them and for me. My parents and grandparents would also be equally satisfied if they could observe.

Jim Rua

Epiphany

My love for food comes from family and personal experiences described in this book. My restaurant vision, my epiphany, came unexpectedly (as epiphanies do) when I was in a strange town, well into adult life. Some time elapsed before I was able to fulfill the dictates of the epiphany.

In 1973, at age thirty-one, I landed a job in Harrisburg, the state capital of Pennsylvania. My friend Jack Gustafson was there working for the Governor's Council on Drug and Alcohol Abuse. Jack had been working with me in New York, where, under Governor Nelson Rockefeller's direction, the State was implementing community-based drug treatment and education programs. I had been working with the State's Narcotic Addiction Control Commission (NACC) since graduation from college in 1967. My responsibilities in New York included supervision of the development of "youthful drug abuse programs," which focused on a growing heroin problem among young people in metropolitan areas. Pennsylvania wished to follow the New York model and hired me as director of the effort.

Jack's father, a hotel and restaurant professional, was staying with my friend when I visited to begin work, prior to moving into a new apartment. I had known Jack's father for many years in Albany, where he was the last manager of the legendary Keeler's State Street Restaurant that closed around 1960. I was always cooking for friends and family in those days, and Jack's father, whom I called Don Juan, frequently encouraged me to go into the restaurant business – usually in jest, but nevertheless he was persistent.

One evening during my visit to Harrisburg, Jack, Don Juan, and I went to an Italian restaurant for drinks and dinner. This place felt to me as if I had conjured it up in a dream: dark wood; decades-old, red leather bar stools; wooden tables with sturdy chairs; arias and Italian art songs playing on the stereo. Best of all, I was treated to the pervasive smell of my dearest childhood culinary recollection: olive oil, garlic, tomatoes, and oregano simmered together as the basis for pizza and pasta sauces, and some antipasti besides. I don't remember the meal we had, but I do remember the joy I felt in that place that was busy with happy guests and good natured staff. I told Jack and the persistent Don Juan that this is the kind of place I would open if I ever got the chance. Jack had a history of working in restaurants as a waiter and bartender, so he was always positive about such fantasies.

The next day I went to work and discovered that a tremendous political upheaval had been announced: the Governor, Milton Schaap, was leaving the next day for the Democratic Presidential Convention in San Francisco, where he had decided to throw his hat into the contest. He was taking with him two of his top aides – the same people who had hired me and had promised to guide me through the rough political situation my arrival would create. I was a young guy from New York hired to run a Pennsylvania bureaucracy about which I knew nothing. The Governor's monumental decision put me in a bind, because I didn't know anybody in the State except the two departing aides, Jack, and his visiting father—Don Juan. I immediately quit the job half way into my first day of work. When I revealed the news to Jack that evening, he quit too. Both of us came back to Albany and Don Juan went home to Florida. Jack resumed his career at NACC.

I arrived home on a bright Sunday morning in the merry month of May without a job or prospects. On Monday I called my friend Jerry Billings, who was Executive Deputy Director of the New York State Office for the Aging and who had been advising me about Harrisburg. Jerry predicted that I might endure an uneasy transition to life in Harrisburg. I wanted to tell him how accurate was his prediction. Fate intervened, however Congress had just authorized a major new program of services for the elderly, and Jerry was seeking to recruit someone to help lead the effort to create "county offices for the aging" across the State. He offered me a job that very day, Assistant Direct of the New York State Office for the Aging, responsible for finance, administration, and development of community based services. Employed again, I started work immediately and remained at the Office for the Aging for the next ten years.

Meanwhile, Jack and I resumed our friendship, and I would occasionally see Don Juan. I continued to cook but had no restaurant plans until one day in the year of our Lord 1976, the owners of Pellegrino Importing Company in Albany–Frank Commisso and Tony Pellegrino–asked me if I would be interested to open a restaurant with them. I called Jack. Bingo, let's do it. I would be in the kitchen, Jack would run the floor and our partners would supply the food.

My next call was to Don Juan in Florida. He took the next plane to Albany and we were in the restaurant business. I swear, Casa Verde, which opened on October 12, 1976, looked and smelled, and felt to me just like that Italian restaurant in Harrisburg. The smells of olive oil, garlic, tomatoes, and oregano permeated the air.

I was advised by a wise man not to quit my day job and I didn't. For the next quarter century I was gainfully employed in two endeavors: service to the people's government by day and the realization of my epiphany by night and on weekends. I retired from state government at the beginning of the millennium and am now devoting full time to my life's work – manifestation of the epiphany.

Intermezzo: Food Story by Jeanette Stanziano

The late *The New York Times* columnist William Safire wrote: "After eating, an epicure gives a thin smile of satisfaction; a gastronome, burping into his napkin, praises the food in a magazine; a gourmet, repressing his burp, criticizes the food in the same magazine; and a gourmand belches happily and tells everybody where he ate; a glutton embraces the white porcelain altar, or, more plainly, he barfs."

Many people come to Café Capriccio's Chef's Table because they consider it a special, intimate destination custom made for food-centric people like themselves. This seems to be true whether they consider themselves gastronomes, gourmands, epicures, gluttons or, a personal favorite, gastronauts. These distinctions among food enthusiasts cause me to wonder at what point in their lives, and under what circumstances, some individuals are struck with a passion for food – the epiphany, the realization that rituals surrounding food production, preparation, and consumption can be among life's great joys.

My friend the noted film critic Amy Biancolli once shared a story with me about her food-related epiphany that occurred unexpectedly when she encountered the great mother of all American food gurus, Julia Child. Amy was a young writer covering an event at Harvard in honor of the celebrated culinarian when she encountered Julia in an elevator on the way to the ceremony. Madam Child was a commanding 6' 2" figure, while Amy stood at a modest 5' 4." Julia appeared to Amy like the Tower of Pisa as she bent slightly towards her and asked the newbie scribe: "Are you a FOOOOOOOOOOD person?" Responding to the culinary maven with signature blunt honesty, Amy replied definitively: "Well, I like to eat!" Without missing a beat, Julia declared, in her natural, percolating and exuberant style: "Well then, you ARRRREEE a food person," thus bestowing a passionate stamp of approval upon the young writer and upon her own revelation that what makes one a food person first and foremost is simply loving to eat.

Most of us do not experience such glitterati moments in our lives leading to culinary love affairs. Many adults, however, can recall pivotal experiences that have influenced a lifelong interest in the lush world of culinary interests.

When I was eleven years old my parents divorced, and my sister Lisa and I spent our allotted weekends with my father, a major-league food enthusiast. Each visit revolved around a special Sunday meal that we shared together, always a happy event and always a serious process. As children we fully participated in all stages of the event, including selecting a menu, shopping, preparation, consumption, and clean up.

On a sunny though bitter February morning in 1971 my father piled Lisa and me into his green Camaro and took off for the local Italian import store to seek provisions for our dinner. My father was an Italian-American version of the Odd Couple's meticulous Felix Unger, crossed with the military background of Robert Duvall's Great Santini. His car was immaculate and we were expected to keep it that way. We pulled into the little shopping plaza where the import store was located as my father instructed us, per usual, to avoid stepping in the oil stains that dotted the parking lot for fear that we would sully the mats in his midlife-mobile. Inside the store, he gently held me by the elbow and steered me against a small open cooler directly inside the door and said, "Stay here and don't touch anything, dolly."

My sister and I were both sporting ugly 1970's winter down coats with too much padding for two little chubby Italianate girls primed to start growing moustaches at any moment. We looked like two dark-eyed meatballs on tooth picks ready to go on the space shuttle into orbit. For about ten minutes we dutifully stood guard by the open cooler, immediately feeling overheated in our puffy coats. Looking over the display, we saw that it contained an assortment of cheeses from around the world. Lisa and I loved cheese, and our family elders taught us that the stinky ones were always the best.

We surveyed the cooler shelves with obedient eyes and spied labels with pictures of goats; red, white, and blue French flags; and for me, the most interesting of all: a bright green shiny-foiled package sitting on the top shelf just out of full view. It called to me like a siren song. DON'T TOUCH ANYTHING kept playing in my Catholic head, but damn, the package was shiny and I just had to know what kind of cheese wore such a splendid, gilded, tempting wrap– and deserved such an elevated spot high above the more common cheeses.

I glanced at my sister and then looked back to the top shelf. Instinctively Lisa said in a matter-of-fact voice: "Don't do it. Dad will KILL YOU!" My father had a fiery temper so I knew that the warning professed real and present danger. For the next five seconds I lowered my head and feigned a study of a mundane Vermont cheddar wrapped in dull green wax while contemplating my moral dilemma and confronting what may have been the groundwork of my first culinary cannon ball. I HAD TO KNOW! I was overcome with the sudden feeling of a personal quest, tantamount to the pursuit of the Holy Grail. Perhaps that shiny green wrapper held the world's most wondrous cheese ever made, certain to transform my life.

CHEESE

The plan was simple: I could look, read, touch, smell, and fondle the cheese; sate my curiosity, and dad would be none the wiser. I wasn't planning the Brinks heist, after all. I would approach the act like a ninja. I looked back up at the top shelf and reached slowly for the object of my desire. Teetering on tippy toes, I placed my fingertips gently on either side of the forbidden object. With fingers delicately in place, I began slowly to tip the cheese towards me to catch a quick glimpse of the label. As I pressed my puffy-parka-clad-belly into the shelves, the cooler filled my nose with a faint sour curd smell. A small alarm went off in my head as I felt the sides of the foil package begin to slip south, lubricated by some moist and slick substance soon to be revealed. The mystery gleaming (now-wet) package slipped from my grasp into sudden mid-air turbulence. In a sort of out-of-body experience I watched the cheese hover over my head, then drop like a smelly, squishy brick, hitting me first on the forehead and then ricocheting off the cooler's second shelf edge before taking a final swan dive directly down my winter jacket, leaving a gross slick of cheese "juice" down the bloated ripples of my parka before reaching its final destination on the floor between my little sister's snow boots. Lisa looked at me with her crazy, Liza Minnelli eyes, and picked up the cheese and threw it back into the cooler like a live grenade without flinching. She said in a deadpan voice: "Limburger, Geez Jeanette, Dad will NEVER KNOW." The big L. The granddaddy of all stinky cheeses. What were the odds? Had some evil cheese-god decided to shorten my childhood? Limburger was the notorious, putrid pride of Belgium, after all. The mystery cheese was respectable but would not transform my life, and could, in fact, abruptly end it once my father "got wind" of my transgression (and I do mean "wind").

Recalling this experience, I now realize that at the tender age of eleven years I was already embarking upon a lifetime of culinary curiosity, willing to risk certain "death" to know what kind of cheese occupied the third shelf of that cooler. There I was, a budding gastronaut quivering in the back seat of my father's once-pristine Camaro. He drove us back to his bachelor pad at an angry speed that I was certain would produce a sonic boom, as he cursed the horrible smell and substance that violated his world, with a few phrases mumbled towards the direction of his disobedient child.

When we returned to my dad's apartment I was instructed by my father to check my cheese-parka at the door before being allowed to enter his man-sanctuary. My dad silently unloaded his take on the counter of his tiny kitchen. As every item was removed from the bag, my father pronounced his new culinary inventory and how it was to be used in our meal. With every description, his mood slowly defrosted. The last item to come out of the bag was a deli package of hot sopressata. My father opened the white paper wrapping and peeled off a slice of the spicy red mottled meat and handed it to me through the little opening of his galley kitchen bar counter. I took a bite of the surprising gift and peaked through at him and smiled as I watched my dad take a slice for himself. As we both felt the fiery salty flavor fill our mouths, we looked at each other and acknowledged its deliciousness, nodding our heads in silent agreement. At that moment, it dawned on me as an eleven-year-old child that food seems to trump all else. Food holds great powers in terms of human interaction. Food is the great equalizer. No matter what the problem or mood, good food is always cause for loving solidarity and a natural coming together of families. No matter how hard the ride was home from the import store, it took just the quiet celebratory moment of unloading one bag of special groceries and two slices of sopressata for an armistice to be reached in the notorious Limburger Incident of 1971. Although my father had been angry, in the end I think he knew more about what I had done and why than I actually did. We shared the same silent approval and camaraderie over the soppresata like a couple of old Italian men on Prince Street. My dad could see that I was a child who had the same love of cooking and food that he did. Perhaps this smelly cheese was wondrous after all.

Fast forward thirty-six years and that same dark-eyed meatball found herself stepping into the subterranean world of Café Capriccio for a maiden dinner on Grand Street. The birthday occasion ended up being a night highlighted by an extraordinary meal, not by candles. Café Capriccio had instantly become my favorite restaurant and piqued my interest to step foot into the door of that restaurant's world.

After a couple of months, one quirky letter sent to the proprietor, and a ten-second follow-up phone call, I found myself hunting down the rare daytime parking spot on Grand Street and traversing the red and green shaky steps up to Jim Rua's unassuming brownstone, home of the Chef's Table. When I arrived Jim greeted me as if we were old friends. He stood at the butcher block in front of his stove, arms wide open, head thrown back with a "aha" face as if to say: "there she is, my old friend Jeanette." I was a total stranger, except for my quirky letter and brief phone conversation expressing interest in his world. Suddenly, I too felt like we were old friends. Jim has the ability to disarm people he meets with a natural spirit of hospitality. My letter expressing personal passion for *la cucina Capriccio* was all that Jim needed to give me a warm greeting and the unmistakable feeling of belonging.

This feeling of inclusion is the signature atmosphere of Café Capriccio's Chef's Table and of Jim himself. Jim not only loves to cook, but as Amy expressed to the legendary Julia with poetic honesty, he loves to eat! We have ordered countless meals in restaurants nearby as well as abroad, where we routinely share three or four appetizers, pasta, and at least one main course. For Jim, a bounteous table reflects the wonder, majesty, and mystery of food and its preparation, along with the simple joy of sharing a splendid meal with loved ones and friends. Now at the Chef's Table, strangers share meals and become part of the family. Many Chef's Table patrons are themselves food explorers, like the great navigators of ancient times, who, when they arrive at Jim's table, consider themselves finally landed – in "a new, pleasant and sometimes unexpected world."

JIM

Jim is a food aficionado on a profoundly simple level. No pretensions, no mystery. Food to Jim is simply the bounty of everything that is readily around us, ripe for the picking. His approach to cooking involves common sense and fearlessness, a love for playing with food, and above all a rejection of affectation and exclusivity. Food is a source of pleasure, simple nourishment, a social framework for family and friends, and an occasion for endless possibilities for creative expression. It is also important to note that a love of eating is required in the world of cooking.

In the years that I have known Jim, I have frequently watched him offer my children food consisting of whatever was in his kitchen, and without regard to the perceived wisdom about children's narrow food preferences. On a quiet winter afternoon in December, my daughter Josie (then ten years old) happily ate two bowls of tripe before she asked what it was. To her, the food simply tasted good, came from Jim (her favorite cook), and she wanted more of it. She was not reluctant to enjoy stomach lining so long as it tasted good. Josie would taste anything that Jim offered her from any mystery pot or sloppy wooden spoon. Young children are fearless by nature, usually willing to try anything, at least once. Children addicted to chicken tenders and mac 'n cheese are more the products of their parents' follies than their own recalcitrant food dispositions.

Jim Rua's encompassing, inclusive, and natural approach to food places him in the same sphere with the young scribe standing in awe of Julia Child and also with the naughty, overstuffed Italian girl of eleven dripping with Limburger juice on her way to a death ride *con queso*. Each of their stories shows a kind of curiosity and fearlessness in the pursuit of culinary interests, and ultimately the enjoyment of food and its wonders. From the open arms of the bearded man meeting a stranger at the Chef's Table or the open mind of youth happily licking fingers from a recent swim in an unknown pot, Julia Child was indeed right about us all. Whether cooking, eating, reading, or blasting off to stars in the endless food galaxy as a card-carrying gastronaut, we are all FOOOOOODDD PEEEEOOOOPPPPPLLLLEEE at heart.

-JS

Organizing a Dinner at the Chef's Table

Guests at Café Capriccio's Chef's Table are offered menu choices that represent a fair sampling of Italian cuisine from different regions, from the Italian Alps to the tip of Sicily. Guests are asked to select five antipasti, one pasta, one main entree, and dessert.

Usually guests allow me to choose the menu based on foods that I am inspired to cook, after spending part of the morning shopping in my favorite markets. Here I emphasize that my shopping for Chef's Table functions includes supermarkets as well as specialty markets such as the Asian groceries, Italian food shops, and the Honest Weight Food Co-op.

Throughout this book I want to emphasize that while the great food we serve at Café Capriccio is usually supplied by wholesale distributors selected for quality and service, I also rely on retail shops, including supermarkets, to gather foods for Chef's Table dinners. I shop at local stores for the following reasons: 1. personal shopping for dinner allows me the flexibility to purchase foods that look best on the day I buy them, and 2. there is an abundance of great food available throughout our community for cooks like you and me. Food procurement in and around the Capital Region is easy; we have ready access to everything we need.

My usual day thus begins finding raw food for the evening's guests, usually from ten to fifteen people. Returning to the kitchen with provisions, I start preparation in the early afternoon for dinner at 6:00 or 7:00 p.m. My first thoughts are about the antipasti selections, which I invariably increase in number from the promised five. Rarely are there fewer than seven antipasti served. First consideration is diversity and balance. Normally I would include individual antipasto preparations of the following types: meatless, meat based, seafood, a green salad, something with cheese, and always grilled vegetables. A typical antipasto assortment at the Chef's Table will include mostly vegetables and salads, some meat, some seafood, and some cheese.

Next is the pasta course. When I am given the discretion to prepare pasta for our guests, I always select a preparation without meat. My rationale is that offering too many varieties of meat and/or serving too much meat is a disservice to the diners. Because our Chef's Table meals are so abundant, we must consider the virtue of light foods and be sparing with foods that are heavy. Pasta with herb-scented tomato sauce, or arugula pesto, or grilled mushrooms is nicely paired with most of the main courses we would select. Some guests select risotto for their pasta course, but I do not prepare risotto unless requested because my impression is that most of our guests will prefer pasta and miss it if it is not included in their meal.

After selecting the pasta, I make preparations for our main course. Sometimes this means preparing a braised dish that requires two or more hours to cook. More often it means trimming and portioning the ingredients which will later be grilled, roasted, or sautéed while guests enjoy the courses that precede it. In the afternoon, I would also prepare vegetables, potatoes, or other accompaniments to the main course.

Finally, dessert: although I am not a dessert maker, we make some of the desserts we serve at Café Capriccio. We also purchase desserts from local pastry chefs who prepare special treats for us, such as ricotta cheesecake. For Chef's Table functions I have been relying upon the brilliant creations of Claudia Crisan and her husband, Ignatius Calabria, whose Crisan Bakery is located nearby.

Following is a typical menu.

ANTIPASTI

Panzanella — Bread Salad from Tuscany

Wild Dandelion Greens with Tomatoes and Fennel

Swiss Chard with Golden Beets 129

Grilled Radicchio with Mushrooms, Parmigiana, and Truffle Oil 57

Pork Tenderloin with Squid Tentacles and Plum Tomatoes on Skewers 70

Frittata with Zucchini Blossoms Stuffed with Ricotta and Basil 74

PASTA

Roasted Sweet Red Pepper Pesto with Tagliatelle 48

MAIN COURSE

Leg of Lamb, Café Capriccio Style, Roasted on the Covered BBQ 107

DESSERT

Sicilian Cheesecake by Danielle Corellis (Café Capriccio Pastry Chef)
and/or Fresh Fruit Tarts from nearby Crisan Bakery

WINES

Pino Grigio, 2008, Villa Puccini

Chianti Rufina, Cedro, 2008, Fattoria Lavacchio

Red Sauce

Just the other day I heard another disparaging remark about the much maligned "red sauce" obsession that seems to affect so many otherwise sensible epicureans. This story involves a notable Italian restaurant owner of Italian origin whose popular restaurant is in a nearby town. The punch line is that the Italian does not serve "red sauce" in his restaurant, lest it be considered beneath the culinary dignity of his clientele.

I have to tell the reader that in thirty years of travel throughout Italy, north, south, east, and west, I can be certain about at least one characteristic of the Italian culinary mindset: every Italian loves tomato sauce with his/her pasta. True, the Ligurian serves basil pesto, the Bolognese serves buttery concoctions, and Alfredo in Rome serves his creamy/cheesy fettuccini. It is, however, indisputable that for Italians macaroni and tomatoes belong together like love and marriage, blue skies and bright sunshine, and big smiles on beautiful faces. The combination of pasta and "sauce" is evidence of God's presence in the world and ultimate compassion for mankind.

Recently I was with a group of travelers in Sicily where we visited the wine estate of *Regaliali*, the home of Anna Tasca Lanza, author of many books about food and *padrona* of a her cooking school at the vineyard. A noble aristocrat by birth and breeding, who died last year after a long life, she was extremely gracious to our travel group. While we were enjoying the fancy dinner prepared by her daughter Fabrizia, Anna told me that however fancy is the feast served to an Italian, what Italians really wish for is a dish of pasta *con salsa di pomodoro*. In her book, *The Heart of Sicily*, Anna says: "Sicilians practically live on spaghetti and tomato sauce; they eat it every day of their life. If you offer them something different, they eat it to please you, all the while longing to get back to their spaghetti."

Some years ago I read a review in *The New York Times* of Italy's first restaurant south of Rome to win three Michelin stars. The restaurant is named Don Alfonso 1890, located in Sant' Agata sui Due Golfi, on the Sorrento peninsula. In this review, the late, eminent R.W. Apple Jr. (Johnny Apple) was accompanied by Faith Willinger, noted food writer and expert on Italian foods. They were served spaghetti graced with strips of San Marzano tomatoes, cooked for a minute with some basil and a little garlic, then spooned over the pasta. Willinger told Apple, "This is the greatest dish on the face of the earth."

I come down solidly on the side of Willinger, Apple, and all the south Italian housewives who annually preserve a winter's worth of fresh tomatoes for sauce soon after August 15, the Feast of the Assumption. Ferragosto signals the end of the summer tomato harvest in the south.

So, what's wrong with the countless Americans who act snarky about the subject of "red sauce"?

Native to South America, the tomato migrated to Europe in the fifteenth century with the new world explorers. The fact that Columbus was Italian, from Genoa, may not be relevant in this discussion, and it may be specious history–but somebody had to preside over the wedding of tomatoes and spaghetti in Napoli, where supposedly it all began so many centuries ago; why not Columbus or one of his crew?

The best tomatoes for "red sauce" come from the lava rich soil around Vesuvius, the menacing volcano that dominates not only the landscape around Napoli but also the attention of all Neapolitan citizens. These tomatoes are named San Marzano after a tiny village near Pompeii named San Marzano sul Sarno, from where the very best are said to originate. Now this variety is grown all around the Campania region, where the sun shines and tomatoes grow for ten months a year.

San Marzano tomatoes are acknowledged to be the best in the world for making "sauce," because they possess perfectly balanced qualities of sweetness and acidity, delicacy and structure, vibrant color and incomparable taste.

My homage to "red sauce" ends with a revelation to readers of this book of a secret ingredient that will improve San Marzano tomato sauce even beyond the powers of Anna Tasca Lanza in Sicily or of the proprietor of Don Alfonso, the imperious Alfonso Iaccarino. Some years ago my friend Jeanette Stanziano brought me a pound of crushed red pepper with the label Utica Grind. This pepper is finely ground and the manufacturers claim that it has "a polished flavor that leaves your mouth watering for more." I believe the combination of San Marzano tomatoes, Utica Grind hot pepper, a hint of garlic, a splash of olive oil, and a few basil leaves will convince even the snarkiest critic that this "red sauce" is indeed "the greatest dish on the face of the earth." And remember when you try this on your foody-elite friends that Utica Grind has been "packaging flabbergasting flavorings for the foodie elite since 1928."

I saw this myself on their web site and know it to be a fact. Many food snobs are sure to be converted if you follow the simple recipe below.

Filetto di Pomodoro
the Mother Sauce with Utica Grind

This is my version of the sauce served to Johnny Apple and Faith Willinger at Don Alfonso 1890: "the greatest dish on the face of the earth!"

Ingredients

2 cans San Marzano tomatoes (each 28 ounces); skins, unripe parts, and other debris removed

4 cloves garlic left whole

4 tablespoons olive oil

½ cup chopped parsley, ½ half cup

chopped basil, salt, and pepper

½ teaspoon Utica Grind hot pepper–more if you have the courage

Pecorino Romano

2 pounds spaghetti

Procedure

Mash the tomatoes with your hands. Don't worry about seeds. Warm the olive oil in a pan until it takes on a hint of color, about 2 minutes. Don't burn the garlic. When the garlic shows a touch of color, take it out of the pan and discard it. Add the tomatoes, salt, hot pepper, and half the basil. Cook the sauce for 5 minutes and then turn off the heat. Now cook the pasta. When the pasta is cooked *al dente,* drain it, toss it in the sauce, turn it into a bowl, and top it with basil and parsley. *Presto*, the greatest dish on the face of the earth!

Pasta

When I opened my first restaurant, Casa Verde, almost thirty-five years ago, I decided to serve only *pasta fatta in casa* (pasta made at home) primarily because it can be cooked quickly. Busy chefs in Italian restaurants don't have time to wait ten minutes for individual orders of pasta to cook, and they sometimes take short cuts by cooking quantities of pasta in advance and then reheating it to order. This is why pasta in restaurants is so often soft and overcooked, and therefore disappointing.

Students of Italian cuisine quickly discover that pasta made at home (typically with eggs added) is usually served for special occasions, often with cream or butter-based sauces. It is also a regional specialty of Emilia Romagna, and its culinary center Bologna. Otherwise, Italians eat dried pasta made from semolina wheat, the harder the better. Pasta lovers in Italy and elsewhere love the firm texture of properly made and cooked semolina pasta. I'm one of those people, and at the Chef's Table I usually serve dried pasta. Of course, at the Chef's Table I'm cooking for a group and not individuals, making the cooking-time factor insignificant.

Concerning brands and labels, there surely are differences in quality from brand to brand, but much of the differences relate to individual preference. My preference is for cooked pasta to be very firm, which some brands cannot achieve because, like minute rice, they are made to be "foolproof." Cook them for a long time or a short time, it doesn't matter – same soft texture.

Most of the Italian labels are superb. I especially like the pasta made in the Campania region (around Naples) along with some of the more famous labels from other regions: De Cecco and Del Verde from Abruzzo, for example. There are many great choices for pasta lovers and the process of investigation is a joy. Each of us is an expert in regard to her/his preferences; the ultimate ratings are therefore strictly subjective and the choices are practically endless. So let the investigation begin – if it hasn't already begun for you.

Despite my stated preference for dried pasta, this chapter will begin with a basic recipe for egg pasta which we use at Café Capriccio when we make it for ourselves. Most of the recipes that follow will anticipate dried pasta but, of course, cooks can choose for themselves which type to prepare. Any sauce in this book will be fine with either fresh or dried pasta.

Recipes that follow will be for ten diners, since this book is primarily about cooking for company. The portions are generous.

Basic Pasta Recipe (2 pounds, made in a mixer)

Ingredients:

2 pounds unbleached all purpose flour

6 medium eggs

1 tablespoon olive oil

pinch of salt

For larger amounts of pasta, use the same proportions and technique below.

Procedure

Beat the eggs. Combine flour and salt in the mixer. Insert the dough hook attachment and start the mixer. Drizzle the egg into the bowl. Mix until ingredients are integrated. Remove dough after it is well mixed and comes together. Add flour as necessary and knead it with your hands for a few minutes. The texture should be sponge-like and slightly moist. Cover the dough and let it rest in the refrigerator for ½ hour. This will relax the dough and make it easier to roll and cut.

Rolling and cutting the dough are important aspects of pasta making. Home cooks can buy small affordable machines that mix dough automatically and extrude it through dies. Commercial pasta is also usually extruded, but commercial pasta is then dried and thus becomes firm. Cooking replaces the water lost in drying, but when cooked properly the dried pasta remains "al dente," firm to the tooth. Freshly made extruded pasta, not allowed to dry, is often soft, lacking substance and texture. This is why I always recommend rolling and cutting fresh pasta, rather than using an extrusion machine. The extrusion method is easier, but the results are not as good.

Cut the dough into manageable portions. Pass it through the rollers of a pasta machine several times, each time reducing the thickness setting. The pasta is ready to be cut when the texture is perfectly smooth and rolled to the desired thickness. Cut the pasta. For ravioli or other stuffed pasta, the setting should be slightly thicker than for long pasta. Stuffed pasta should be cooked quickly or frozen because the stuffing will quickly saturate the pasta if allowed to stand for more than a few minutes. Frozen, the stuffed pasta will last for months.

Unstuffed pasta can be held in the refrigerator for at least one day, provided it is dusted with semolina to prevent sticking. You may also freeze it, later cooking it from the frozen state.

Cooking time for stuffed pasta is several minutes; for unstuffed pasta, only a couple of minutes in rapidly boiling salted water.

Pasta with Tuna, Tomatoes, Olives, Anchovies, and Capers

For families who love pasta with the briny taste of olives and the seashore, this is a wonderful dish with roots in the south of Italy. Anywhere from Naples to Sicily, and always along the coast, a lucky traveler is likely to find variations on this kind of bountiful creation, especially in the small, family-operated trattorias ubiquitous throughout the south. The recipe below is suggestive of Puttanesca from Naples, with the addition of canned tuna for which the Italians have high regard. Serve it with tossed salad, crunchy bread, and a light dessert for a great late-afternoon Sunday supper.

INGREDIENTS

2 cans San Marzano tomatoes (each 28 ounces); skins, stems, and debris removed

3 cans tuna in water (each 5 ounces)

1 cup calamata olives, chopped

3 tablespoons capers

1 small can anchovies packed in oil

6 cloves chopped garlic

2 tablespoons dried oregano

Olive oil

Hot pepper flakes to taste (I use Utica Grind)

Chopped parsley

2 pounds pasta (penne rigate)

PROCEDURE

Bring 4 to 5 quarts of salted water to a boil for the pasta.

Heat anchovies and the oil in which they are packed together with olive oil for 1 minute. Add garlic and sauté for about 1 minute, without burning the garlic. Crush the tomatoes, add to the ingredients, stir, combine everything else, and simmer for 15 to 20 minutes. Turn off the pot and let the sauce rest.

Cook the pasta. This will take less than 10 minutes. Drain the pasta when it's done to your liking, return it to the pasta-pot, and add the sauce, tossing to cover the pasta without drowning it. Allow the pasta and sauce to mingle for a couple of minutes so that the pasta absorbs some of the sauce. Pour the pasta into a large serving bowl and bring it to the convivial table.

Ragu of Boar (Cinghiale Fiorentina)

Ingredients

16 ounces ground boar
(or pork if you cannot find boar)

1 chopped onion

6 cloves chopped garlic

2 cups chopped carrot

2 cups chopped celery

½ cup chopped fresh fennel

1 cup red wine

Parmigiano cheese, grated

1 can San Marzano tomatoes

(28 ounces), skins, stems,
and debris removed

2 tablespoons tomato paste

1 teaspoon rosemary

Chopped parsley

4 tablespoons olive oil

Salt and pepper

2 pounds pasta (wide noodles are
especially good for this preparation;
try pappardelle)

Procedure

Sauté the onion in olive oil for a couple of minutes. Add the meat and vegetables and sauté for about 7 minutes. Add the wine and reduce it for about 5 minutes. Add the tomatoes and tomato paste, herbs, and spices. Let the sauce cook slowly for at least 1 hour. When the sauce is finished, cook the pasta in plenty of boiling water, then toss it into the sauce for a couple of minutes. Turn it into a serving dish and serve garnished with Parmigiano and chopped parsley.

Nero di Sepia
(Squid in Black Ink, also known as Calamari Neri)

Sepia (or cuttlefish) is a squid variety characterized by plump flesh, a true backbone and a large ink sac delicious in various sauces. Italian cuisine usually features sepia combined with rice in a dish called *risotto con nero di sepia*. Rarely does one find ink sauce served with pasta, although I have seen it in the deep south of Italy and in Sicily. At Café Capriccio, we have been serving *calamari neri* with pasta for our entire history. The best place to find sepia is in Asian markets. These fish are usually cleaned, however, and do not include the ink sacs, essential for this preparation. In recent years the ink has been sold separately in specialty stores and in some fish markets. Squid ink can also be found online from specialty purveyors.

Ingredients

12 ounces of cuttlefish, cleaned and cut into serving pieces

8 tablespoons squid ink

1 can San Marzano tomatoes (28 ounces)

1 cup white wine

4 ounces tomato paste

1 small can anchovies

2 tablespoons olive oil

1 small diced onion

1 small diced red pepper (sweet)

6 cloves chopped garlic

½ teaspoon ground coriander

2 tablespoons capers

2 pounds pasta (spaghetti is a good choice)

Preparation

Sauté onions and peppers in olive oil for 3 to 5 minutes. Add garlic and sauté for another minute. Add sepia and sauté for several minutes. Add anchovies, tomatoes, squid ink, tomato paste, wine, coriander, and capers, and simmer for 15 minutes, after which the sauce should be rich and black. Cook spaghetti until al dente. When the spaghetti is cooked, toss with the sauce so that all ingredients are thoroughly integrated. Transfer to bowls and serve.

Meat Sauce Bolognese Style

Ingredients

1½ pounds chopped meat (veal, pork, and beef are a good combination)

2 ounces chopped pancetta (bacon from the pig's belly found in Italian delis)

1 chopped onion

2 cups chopped carrot

2 cups chopped celery

1 can San Marzano tomatoes (28 ounces); skins, stems, and debris removed

1 can tomato paste (6 ounces)

8 ounces beef broth

1 cup milk

½ teaspoon nutmeg

½ teaspoon fresh or dried sage

Parmigiano cheese

Chopped parsley

Olive oil

Salt and pepper

2 pounds pasta (fresh egg pasta would be a good choice; try pappardelle or fettuccini)

Procedure

Sauté the onion and vegetables in olive oil and pancetta for several minutes, until the onion shows a bit of color. Add the meat and vegetables and sauté for about 10 minutes. Add the tomatoes, broth, tomato paste, milk, herbs, and spices. Let the sauce cook for a couple of hours at very low heat. When the sauce is finished, cook the pasta, then toss in the sauce and serve in a beautiful bowl with Parmigiano and parsley.

Sauce Bechamel (The Italians call it Balsamella)

This is a basic cream/flour/butter sauce that is particularly good when combined with vegetables or seafood such as shrimp and scallops. It can also stand on its own and serve as a simple sauce for pasta.

1 quart milk	Salt
4 tablespoons flour	Parmigiano cheese
4 tablespoons butter	Chopped parsley
	2 pounds pasta

Procedure

Combine flour, milk, butter, and salt in a pot. Bring the contents to a simmer, stirring all the while. When all ingredients are integrated and the sauce is smooth, the béchamel is finished, in about 10 minutes.

Cook 2 pounds of pasta in boiling water until al dente. Drain the pasta, toss with the béchamel, finish with Parmigiano and parsley. Turn into a bowl and serve.

Pomodorini (Fresh Cherry or Grape Tomatoes)

Ingredients

2 pounds cherry tomatoes, cut in half

6 cloves minced garlic

5 tablespoons olive oil

Fresh basil, chopped

Parsley, chopped

Salt and pepper

Parmigiano cheese

2 pounds pasta (thin spaghetti is particularly good with this light sauce)

Procedure

Sauté the garlic for a minute. Add tomatoes and salt and cook for only a few minutes more. Add the basil at the end.

Cook the pasta in plenty of water and toss into the sauce. Finish with plenty of chopped fresh basil and parsley with Parmigiano for those who wish it.

Clams with Olive Oil & Garlic (alle Vongole)

Ingredients

3 dozen littleneck clams

3 ounces olive oil

6 cloves chopped garlic

¼ teaspoon hot pepper

Juice from 3 lemons

2 tablespoons chopped basil

2 tablespoons chopped parsley

2 pounds pasta (linguine works just fine)

Procedure:

Scrub the clams. Place clams in a large sauté pan without stacking them. If you must lay them on top of each other do so, but the pan will be crowded when the clams open and the final stages of preparation will be more difficult. Add olive oil and cook covered over moderate heat.

After about 3 minutes, when the clams begin to exude their juices, add the garlic, shake the pan, and cover again. Continue cooking for approximately 5 minutes, until most of the clams are opened. The freshest clams will produce the most liquid, and will take longer to open. Be vigilant to monitor progress. If the clams you use do not contain much liquid, or if you cook them too fast, the clam juice will evaporate and your sauce will be disappointing.

Add the herbs when most of the clams are open, reserving half of the parsley. Herbs should not cook for more than a few minutes, after which they rapidly lose their potency. When the clams are open, add the lemon juice to the broth. It is best to allow all clams to open naturally in the pan, rather than to force them open. Partially cooked clams will not consolidate in their shells and won't present the same plump and juicy texture as their companions.

Before tossing pasta in the sauce, place the clams around the rim of individual platters. Add a splash of broth and a sprinkle of parsley to each clam. Cook the pasta so that it comes out at about the time the sauce is ready. Toss the cooked pasta in clam broth, allowing the pasta to absorb as much as sauce as possible. Serve the pasta in the center of the platter, clams surrounding it, with parsley generously applied; add lemon wedges for garnish.

Puttanesca

This is how I observed maestro Gaetano Fazio prepare puttanesca in his restaurant on the island of Ischia, where puttanesca is said to have originated. There is some controversy about the origin of this sauce, named after ladies of the night. Some say that its name derives from the quick and easy method of preparation favored by "working girls"; some say it is hot and spicy like its namesake; some refuse to speculate, preferring merely to enjoy it.

Ingredients

2 cans San Marzano tomatoes (each 28 ounces); cores and skins removed, coarsely chopped

8 cloves minced garlic

4 tablespoons olive oil

Anchovies – at least 2 per person – mashed

2 tablespoons capers

1½ cups Mediterranean olives, such as calamata, chopped, with pits removed

Crushed red pepper to taste (Utica Grind is always my choice)

Chopped basil

Chopped parsley

Salt and pepper

2 pounds pasta (ziti or penne are good choices)

Procedure

Sauté garlic in olive oil with anchovies for a minute. Don't burn the garlic. Add tomatoes, capers, olives, crushed pepper, and half of the fresh herbs and stir. Simmer for 10 to 15 minutes, uncovered. When the sauce is ready, it should be fairly thick, and a little dark from the olive influence.

Cook the pasta and drain it. Return the drained pasta to the pot in which it was cooked, ladle some sauce over the pasta, and toss it thoroughly so that the pasta is coated. Now place the pasta into a serving bowl, and spoon a little sauce on top with parsley. Serve extra sauce on the side. No cheese.

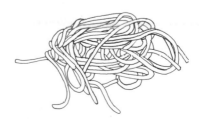

Frutta di Mare (Mixed Fish & Shellfish)

Frutta di mare is a festive dish, which can include a variety of fish and shellfish. This is a dish to serve on Christmas Eve when the theme is fish and shell fish.

The cook's primary objectives are

1. to coordinate the cooking time of each fish so that none is undercooked and none overcooked when the pasta is ready to be served; and

2. to produce a sauce whose texture is appropriate for pasta, rather thick and not soup-like.

Ingredients

1 dozen littleneck clams (smaller clams for this recipe because you will need space in your pan for other ingredients)

1 dozen black mussels, beards removed and shells scrubbed

10 large sea scallops

8 ounces calamari, cleaned, body cut into rings and tentacles chopped

10 large shrimp, no smaller than 15 to the pound; cleaned, with the tail segment left on the shrimp

3 cups San Marzano tomatoes, cores and seeds removed, coarsely chopped

6 cloves chopped garlic

Chopped basil

Chopped parsley

1 teaspoon of hot pepper (Utica Grind)

2 tablespoons capers

½ cup pitted olives chopped

2 pounds pasta (linguine, tagliatelle, or fettuccine)

Procedure

Shrimp should be sliced down their back to remove the vein and to create a "butterfly" effect when cooked. Slice through about one quarter of the shrimp's body.

In a pan large enough to hold the fish and the sauce, sauté garlic in olive oil for about 1 minute over moderate heat. Add the tomatoes and bring to a simmer. Add the clams in their shells; cook covered for about 4 minutes. Add the mussels, calamari, and scallops and continue to simmer uncovered for 3 minutes. Add the shrimp and herbs (reserve some parsley for later) and cook until the shrimp are brightly colored and firm, about 3 minutes.

Time your pasta so that it is cooked al dente about 2 minutes after the shrimp are firm and bright. Meanwhile, during the last two minutes of pasta cooking time, arrange the shellfish around the perimeter of a large serving platter. Reserve some sauce on the side, toss the pasta in the sauce, and place the pasta in the center of the platter with shrimp, scallops, and calamari on top. Sprinkle with parsley and basil all around.

A Parade of Pestos

Following are several pesto preparations that will glorify your chef's table. Pesto is often associated with the basil sauce from Genoa, *pesto alla Genovese*, but imaginative cooks can create endless pesto variations to adorn their pasta selections. The ingredients for recipes that follow will include vegetables and herb combinations, usually, although not always, with nuts or seeds to provide crunch. Pesto needs crunch.

The term pesto is based on the Italian verb *pestare* which means "to pound,"or "to grind," a process that occurs in a mortar and pestle – the traditional method for preparing pesto sauce. Today I use a food processor to prepare many varieties of pesto for Chef's Table dinners.

My food processor is a basic Cuisinart with two functions: a high speed that will puree virtually anything with moisture content, and a pulsating function that is just right for pesto. Pesto should always possess a substantive texture with its individual ingredients recognizable. The texture of pesto should never be puree.

Once prepared, pesto is not cooked, or heated on the stove. It is added to steaming pasta and tossed vigorously to integrate it thoroughly. I sometimes add a little heavy cream to facilitate integration of whatever pesto I have created. If cream is to be added, I heat it first. The cream disappears and is primarily intended as an aid for distribution, so that all of the pasta served is evenly dressed with its pesto adornment. One can also add some of the salted water in which the pasta was cooked to facilitate the pesto-saucing process.

The recipes that follow assume that two cups of finished pesto will be sufficient for one pound of pasta, four cups for two pounds. Once the pasta is dressed with its pesto sauce, additional pesto is not added—unlike liquid sauces. Be sure therefore to adequately dress the pasta you serve.

When feeding a crowd at your chef's table I recommend selecting short cuts of pasta that can be easily handled by guests and whose shapes will accept the sauce. Recommended pasta shapes for pesto include farfalle, gemelli, small shells, short fusilli, and mini penne rigate. Larger cuts such as rigatoni or standard penne rigate are less desirable; and spaghetti, while perfect for groups of two or four, is unwieldy for a crowd of ten.

Cooking pasta for pesto preparations

Cook the pasta to the desired texture. Drain the pasta, then return it to the still-hot pot in which it was cooked, leaving a bit of salted hot water in as well. This will facilitate distribution of the sauce. Toss the pesto into the pasta and stir vigorously. When the pesto and pasta appear as a conjugal couple, turn it into a bowl and serve. The preparations that follow can be served hot or warm and are also good at room temperature.

All pesto recipes that follow will produce two cups of finished pesto, enough for one pound of pasta. Adjust ingredients proportionally for larger quantities.

Pesto alla Genovese

Ingredients

4 cups packed basil leaves

½ cup pine nuts

3 cloves garlic

1 cup grated Pecorino Romano

Olive oil

Procedure

Toast the pine nuts until they show a little color. This can be done in the oven or in a sauté pan with a tablespoon of olive oil. Do not burn the pine nuts. Neither should you use them raw, as they are then quite bland.

Using a food processor, grind the garlic and pine nuts together using the pulsing function. Add basil and other ingredients, including the olive oil.

Pulse the food processor until all ingredients are blended and form a substantial texture. I recommend pouring a cup of olive oil into the food processor at this stage of preparation. Add more oil if necessary as you proceed. Let the pesto stand for at least 1 hour, after which it is ready to use.

Cook 1 pound of pasta and toss with pesto as described previously.

Pesto with Arugula, Spinach, Sun-Dried Tomatoes, and Feta

Ingredients

2 cups packed arugula

2 cups packed spinach

1 cup unsalted almonds

3 cloves garlic

¾ cup feta cheese, crumbled

½ cup sun-dried tomatoes packed in oil

1 cup olive oil

Procedure

Using a food processor, grind the garlic and almonds together using the pulsing function. Add arugula, spinach, basil, and other ingredients, including the olive oil. Pulse the food processor until all ingredients are blended and form a substantial texture. Add more oil if necessary.

Let the pesto stand for at least 1 hour, after which it is ready to use.

You should be able to see tiny bits of sun-dried tomato along with the colors of the other ingredients.

Cook 1 pound of pasta and toss with pesto as described above.

Olive/Pepper Tapanade Pesto

Ingredients

4 large red bell peppers

1 cup calamata olives, pitted

1 small can anchovies

4 cloves garlic, chopped

¼ cup capers

Pinch of hot pepper (Utica Grind)

¾ cup olive oil

Procedure

Roast the peppers. Burn the skin by cooking them over a gas fire. When the skin is black, cool the pepper, and then run it under cold water, removing the skin and core. Place all ingredients into a food processor. Pulse to integrate all ingredients. Let the mixture stand for at least 1 hour, after which the pesto is ready to use. The color should show the dark olive aspect, but also the color of the peppers.

Cook 1 pound of pasta and toss with pesto as described above.

Sweet Roasted Red Pepper Pesto

Ingredients

5 large red bell peppers

4 cloves garlic, chopped

¾ cup Pecorino Romano, grated

½ cup pistachio nuts

Chopped parsley

Pinch of hot pepper (Utica Grind)

Olive oil

Procedure

Roast the peppers. Burn the skin by cooking them over a gas fire. When the skin is black, cool the pepper, then run under cold water, removing the skin and core. Place all ingredients into a food processor. Pulse to integrate all ingredients. Let stand for at least 1 hour, after which the pesto is ready to use.

Cook 1 pound of pasta and toss with pesto as described above.

Pesto di Cavolo Nero (Tuscan Kale)

Note that the kale is steamed first in order to tenderize it.

Ingredients

4 cups Tuscan Kale, large stalks removed, leaves separated, and roughly chopped

½ cup salted sunflower seeds

4 cloves garlic

1 cup Pecorino Romano, grated

1 cup olive oil

Procedure

Steam the kale for 5 minutes until it is quite soft. Let the kale cool.

In a food processor, grind the garlic and sunflower seeds together, using the pulsing function. Add kale and other ingredients, including the olive oil. Pulse the food processor until all ingredients are blended and form a substantial texture. Let the pesto stand for at least 1 hour, after which it is ready to use.

Cook 1 pound of pasta and toss with pesto as described above.

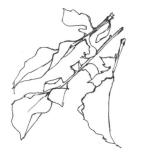

Tomato Pesto with Unsalted Nuts

Ingredients

6 ounces tomato paste

3 cups San Marzano tomatoes

½ cup unsalted nuts

4 cloves garlic

¾ cup ricotta salata, grated

Additional ricotta salata for dressing the finished pasta

Chopped basil

Chopped parsley

1 cup olive oil

Procedure

After removing skins, stems and debris that may be in the can, crush the tomatoes. In a food processor, grind the garlic and nuts using the pulsing function. Add all other ingredients and process until blended. The finished texture should be firm but not stiff. Let stand for 1 hour.

Cook 1 pound of pasta and toss with pesto.

Finish with grated ricotta salata cheese, basil, and parsley.

Radicchio Rosso Pesto with Potatoes and Green Beans

Ingredients

2 heads radicchio rosso, chopped

½ cup salted pumpkin seeds

4 cloves garlic

¾ cup Pecorino Romano, grated

1 cup olive oil

8 ounces French style green beans

2 red skin potatoes

Chopped parsley

Procedure

Steam the green beans until cooked, about 3 to 4 minutes. Set them aside.

Dice the potato in bite-sized pieces. Steam the potatoes until tender, about 3 minutes. Set aside with the green beans. In a food processor, grind the garlic with pumpkin seeds. Add the radicchio, Pecorino, and olive oil.

Process until all ingredients are blended, using the pulsing function. Set the pesto aside for at least 1 hour.

Cook 1 pound of pasta, then toss in the pesto and distribute evenly. Add the beans and potatoes. Turn onto a platter (or into a bowl) and top with Pecorino.

WHERE CAN YOU BUY GOOD FOOD

At lunch in Palermo I was sitting one fine day enjoying the company of one of our holiday travelers. We were staying at a regal hotel in the center of town with a fabulous rooftop restaurant that featured open sides, offering a panoramic view of the city. She was rhapsodizing over the pasta course and said to me, "this pasta is fantastic. Too bad we can't get it at home. How do they do it?" "I'll tell you," I said. "It's made with canned tomatoes, olive oil, garlic, basil, a pinch of hot pepper, and a can of tuna fish, the kind you can buy in any grocery store. It takes about ten minutes to prepare. I'll make it for you when we get home." Incredulous she was, and I think a little disappointed.

A mystique about the origins of the good food glorifies the dishes we enjoy most in the best restaurants. I hear it all the time: these lentils you serve are so delicious, surely they must come from some special place in Umbria where the exotic lentil is cultivated. Or, where could rice in this risotto you serve possibly be found, so sublime in flavor, so plump and colorful? You must have a special supply line from to Po Valley itself, like the ancient spice routes to and from the Orient. Or, where can I buy this very Swiss chard, green like spring, and these golden beets you serve with it, the color of sunshine? Where can these marvels of nature be found by ordinary people who love to cook and to eat?

The first place to look is in your local supermarket. The variety of foods now available in every supermarket is astonishing. The supermarket is indeed the land of milk and honey for home cooks and a paradise for food lovers. Modern production methods, rapid distribution systems, and advanced preservation techniques ensure abundant supplies of everything perishable. The key element to consider as a consumer when shopping for perishables is turnover. The big and busy stores have huge and rapid turnover of products that helps to assure freshness and quality. Customers in supermarkets can actually select the foods they buy, and reject selections that cry to be rejected; in this regard the supermarket is the culinary equivalent of the Athenian democratic experience: everyone gets to vote and does vote in his/her own interest and in the interest of everyone else at his/her table.

Canned and other preserved foods of every taste and description are conspicuously available in supermarkets. Is there any dried bean variety unavailable? Nuts, dried fruits, grains, macaroni products, olive and other oils from everywhere, spices and herbs, countless brands of tomatoes, olives galore, anchovies, capers....Could anything be missing from the shelves of your local super? The answer is a qualified yes, some foods are missing. What and where would they be?

My favorite alternative shopping emporium is our local Asian superstore. Here we find foods that occidentals can only speculate about. Fifty or more varieties of fish are available either fresh on ice or still swimming in tanks; twice as many species are available frozen. Where else does the Italian cook find *sepia*, the large squid also called cuttlefish with a backbone birds like to peck and a large ink sack for making delicious pasta and rice dishes? Where else do we find razor clams and Manila clams that look and taste like the Mediterranean specimens called *vongole*? Smelts and tiny fish for *frittura di pesce* are piled high under ice next to *scungilli*, which are delicious in seafood salads; crates of fresh oysters tempt the shopper; mussels and clams are continuously bathed with sea water to keep fresh. This Asian market is state of the art and filled with good things for *bouillabaisse, zarzuela de mariscos, cioppino di pesce, zuppa di pesce, cacciuccco Livornese* and whatever other names are given to the glorious fish stews we find in cuisines from many lands.

Green vegetables sold in Asian stores are as plentiful as they are mysterious. I have a particular love for Chinese broccoli, with its wide and delicious stalks, and for long beans that the Italians call *serpenti,* as if named for small serpents found in many gardens. Fresh and delicious greens for soups and sautés are abundantly displayed in the Asian markets and are worth discovering. Take a chance when you next make vegetable soup or sauté greens with olive oil and garlic: buy something in the Asian market that looks fresh and delectable. You won't be disappointed–just remember the name of it for future reference.

Many Asian stores also sell meats not available in supermarkets. Pork bellies, for example, are in my local market, as well as every part of the pig from the snout to the tail. Rabbit, quail, duck, duck and quail eggs, fruits and other vegetables, mushrooms, herbs and spices, chili peppers– Asian markets are great sources for home cooks who wish to venture beyond the realm of ordinary experience.

The Honest Weight Food Co-op, or a co-op in your community, is another source for foods that may not be found in the supermarket. Suffice to say here that if a cook is seeking organic fruits and vegetables, free range eggs, locally produced meats, grains of all kinds, and the best selection of cheese in the area, the Co-op should be on your list of sources.

And finally, at Café Capriccio we use a few products that are hard to find, even in our favorite shops and markets. For example, we often "import" salami from places in Brooklyn, Astoria, or from Arthur Avenue in the Bronx. Some items we now make in-house: Cotechino sausage, for example, is available from Arthur Avenue in the Bronx—and now Franco makes it for Café Capriccio.

The overarching point I wish to make for the home cook is that the great foods we use at Café Capriccio for your favorite dishes are under your nose in the big supermarkets, the Co-op, the Asian markets, and the small Italian groceries in our community. Cooks who live in these parts, me included, have just about everything we need at the end of a ten-minute drive.

GRILL IT

There is no more satisfying food related recollection for me than imagining again my father, handsome and vigorous in his middle years, grilling the family's supper on a Sunday afternoon. My father's grill was a one dimensional, three-legged-product sold for a couple of bucks at the local hardware store. The vivid image I have of dad grilling is more than fifty years old but I can still smell the fire and taste the cooking.

Today the simple grill has been replaced by a myriad of devices that include gas and electric grills, char broilers using propane and natural gas, brick ovens in back yards that accept iron grates placed over hot coals, stove top grills named gratellae, rotisseries, smokers, devices that attach to the back of cars for use in parking lots at football games and car races, kettle cookers, and more. All of them work magic depending on what you're cooking, where you're cooking it, and what culinary results you are seeking. Recipes that follow can be applied for use on most of the above equipment.

We serve grilled foods at the Chef's Table throughout the year. Weather permitting, we use an outdoor barbeque where we cook over wood. Otherwise, we employ our char broiler inside – which we regularly use to prepare vegetables. We also use a heavy cast iron ridged skillet called a gratella that is heated on the stove. The gratella provides excellent results, and several preparations in this book are tailored to it.

THE IMPORTANT CONSIDERATIONS WHEN GRILLING INCLUDE THE FOLLOWING DETAILS:

Select a grill that is suited to your environment and cooking objectives. If you're camping with a small group, a small Weber kettle may be just right. If you are grilling for a crowd, something larger would be necessary.

Consider using a grill with a dome when you can. Most grilled foods benefit from domed cooking because the dome intensifies heat, retards fare ups, and permits circulation of smoke that gives great flavor to meat, fish, and vegetables.

Create a hot fire using regular charcoal, hardwood lump charcoal, or if you have dried hardwood, you can use that. Wood chips that impart the special flavors of mesquite, oak, or hickory are also good, sprinkled over regular charcoal. Wood chips must always be soaked before adding to the fire. Soaking will create flavorful smoke and prevent the chips from quickly incinerating.

Start the fire by lighting non toxic paraffin starters under the charcoal; or by using a small "chimney" device that holds charcoal in a cylinder under which is placed lighted newspaper; or by building a "brush fire" under charcoal with dried brush, wood fragments, or old vines. Never use lighter fluid. Not only will the chemicals affect the taste but they are also unhealthy.

Season your grilled foods sparingly before cooking and do not coat them with excess marinade or oils. Oily liquid will cause flare ups than can be too intense, scorch the food, and harm the cook. Be careful.

Begin grilling after the charcoal or wood is reduced to hot coals. Do not grill over an open flame, and be sure the grill is hot before you cook on it.

Be careful to grill where there is plenty of ventilation, to avoid the hazards of carbon monoxide; one such hazard is the untimely demise of the cook.

Don't be afraid to burn the foods you grill a little so that they show the marks of the fire.

Grilled Radicchio with Mushrooms, Parmigiano, and Truffle Oil

This salad looks beautiful and contains a stunning variety of complementary tastes, accentuated by the grilled vegetables.

Ingredients

Radicchio (calculate ¼ head of radicchio for each guest)

Portobello mushrooms (½ mushroom cap per guest)

Imported Parmigiano cheese

Truffle oil, black or white

Salt and pepper

Procedure

Cut the radicchio into fairly thick sections (half-inch slices if using the round variety – cut lengthwise in half if using Treviso). Toss the radicchio with olive oil and grill it for a few minutes, turning frequently. The objective is to burn and flavor the surface, not to cook it through. After grilling, set the radicchio aside.

Grill the mushrooms for several minutes until they begin to wilt. This will take 3 to 5 minutes depending on the heat source. When finished grilling, let the mushrooms cool.

Cut the radicchio into salad-sized pieces. Cut the mushrooms correspondingly. Season with salt and pepper, then toss the salad with truffle oil. Finish with thin slices of Parmigiano on top.

Grilled Mushrooms with Pumpkin (or Squash) and Scallions

King oyster mushrooms are available in Asian markets. They are long and firm, about 2 inches in circumference and 5 to 6 inches long. One mushroom can serve 4 to 5 guests.

Ingredients

Whole portobello mushrooms; calculate ½ mushroom cap per guest

King oyster mushrooms; calculate 1 for 4 to 5 guests

Pumpkin or butternut squash, outer skin removed; calculate ½ the volume of the mushrooms, e.g., 1 pound of mushrooms, ½ pound pumpkin

Scallions, trimmed and washed

Olive oil

Salt and pepper

Procedure

Clean the portobello mushrooms, leaving them whole. Slice the oyster mushrooms lengthwise into pieces about ¼ inch thick. Cut the pumpkin into pieces large enough to fit on the grill and not fall through the cracks. Trim the scallions. Toss the vegetables in a little olive oil with salt to taste.

Grill the vegetables, turning frequently to prevent overcooking. The cooking process should take about 10 minutes. The scallions will cook first, next the mushrooms, and then the pumpkin. After the mushrooms are cool enough to handle, cut them as you wish. Cut the grilled pumpkin in pieces roughly similar to the mushrooms. Add the scallions. Artfully arrange everything on a platter.

GRILLED MUSHROOMS WITH ARUGULA AND PARMIGIANO

INGREDIENTS

Portobello mushrooms (1 per person)

Other mushroom varieties as you like: oyster mushrooms, for example

Fresh arugula (½ cup per person)

Parmigiano

Salt and pepper

Olive oil

PROCEDURE

Grill the mushrooms whole for about 5 minutes, turning them a few times.

Clean and dry the arugula. Place the arugula in a salad bowl. When the mushrooms are cool, cut them, and add to the arugula. Season with salt and pepper, and then toss with olive oil. Finish the salad with thin slices of Parmigiano distributed throughout.

GRILLED ARTICHOKES WITH OLIVE OIL AND LEMON

Here is an easy and unconventional way to prepare a delicious artichoke appetizer. We boil whole, untrimmed, artichokes in water for about 10 minutes. When they are cool we trim them, cut them into quarters, marinate, and then grill them, preferably over wood.

Fresh artichokes come in different sizes that require different treatments. For example, large artichokes contain a prickly choke in the center that must be removed, while the center of the smallest varieties are completely edible. Americans don't love artichokes as much as the Italians do, especially the Romans; artichokes are ubiquitous on Roman menus.

The Italian love for artichokes is reflected in the familial way they are named: the largest are called *mamma*, smaller varieties are called *figli* (children), and the smallest are named *nipoti* (nephews). I imagine a children's fable featuring the artichoke family, *mamma*, *figli*, and *nipoti*, perhaps living in a forest near Winnie the Pooh.

INGREDIENTS

Whole artichokes (½ per person)

2 lemons, cut into quarters

FOR THE MARINADE:

4 cloves garlic

½ teaspoon dried oregano

Juice of 2 lemons

Salt and pepper

½ cup of olive oil

PROCEDURE

To make ½ cup of marinade, finely chop the garlic, add olive oil, lemon juice, and seasonings. Whisk to integrate all ingredients.

Boil the artichokes in lightly salted water until they are cooked through, about 10 minutes for very large artichokes, less time for smaller specimens. Allow the artichokes to cool, then trim the tops and then cut into quarter pieces. Leave the tough outer leaves intact; they will hold the artichokes together. Remove the choke from the center, if necessary.

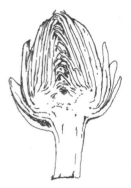

Drizzle the marinade throughout the inner parts and let them stand for a while. Grill the artichokes over coals for several minutes, turning a few times. Grill the lemon quarters at the same time as the artichokes. Arrange the artichokes on a platter, garnished with grilled lemons.

Fennel, Orange, Olive and Sweet Onion Grill

Ingredients

Whole fennel bulbs, stems removed; calculate 1 average-sized bulb for 4 guests

Orange slices, 2 per person

Rind from the above oranges

Calamata or other black olives, a few for each guest

1 sweet onion

Olive oil

Chopped parsley

Salt and pepper

Procedure

Cut the fennel bulb lengthwise into ¼ inch thick pieces, leaving the root intact. This will hold the fennel together. Extract the orange rind with an appropriate kitchen gadget. A potato peeler will work, but a "zester" is best for this purpose.

Slice the oranges and trim away the white part. Brush olive oil on the fennel and grill it for 3 minutes on each side. Brush olive oil on the oranges and grill them on one side only just long enough to mark them. Slice a sweet onion paper-thin. When the fennel is ready, arrange slices on a platter (they can be cut in half or quarters) garnished with oranges (grilled side up), olives, and onion slices. Finish with parsley, orange rind, and olive oil.

Asparagus Grilled on Top of the Stove with Smoked Salmon

The stove top grill (*gratella*) is one of the best vehicles for preparing asparagus. This preparation includes smoked salmon. It is quick, easy, colorful, and delicious.

Ingredients

Fresh asparagus, 4 to 6 pieces for each person

Smoked salmon, about 1 ounce for each person

Chopped garlic

Olive oil

Lemons, lemon juice, and lemon zest

Salt and pepper

Procedure

Wash the asparagus and trim the bottoms. Toss the asparagus in olive oil with a pinch of salt. Heat the gratella, then grill the asparagus for 3 to 5 minutes. The asparagus should be firm. Add garlic for the last minute of cooking. Add lemon juice at the end. Arrange the grilled asparagus in the center of a platter with pieces of salmon arranged around the rim. Garnish the asparagus with lemon wedges and lemon zest.

GRILLED PEARS WITH PROSCIUTTO AND GOAT CHEESE

This recipe uses the stove top grill (*gratella)* which works well for grilling fruit.

INGREDIENTS

Ripe pears, cored and sliced about ¼ inch; calculate ½ pear per person

Sliced prosciutto, calculate about 2 slices per person

Goat cheese, 1 ounce per person

Olive oil

Lemon wedges

Chopped parsley

PROCEDURE

Heat the grill pan. Brush the pears with olive oil. Grill the pears for about 1 minute on each side. The pears should remain firm with the outer surfaces slightly caramelized. Allow the pears to cool. Arrange them on a platter leaving space for the prosciutto. Fold thin slices of prosciutto around the pears. Slice or crumble the goat cheese and arrange it around the other ingredients. Garnish with lemon wedges and parsley.

Grilled Flank Steak with Grilled Mango

This is a substantial dish with an interesting contrast of tastes and textures. One would not normally find this upon an Italian table, since the mango is indigenous to India, far from the Mediterranean. Nevertheless, it fits nicely into the *agrodolce* traditions of Italian and other Mediterranean cuisines. Flank steak is a thin slab of beef from the hindquarter. The flank you buy will weigh a pound or more. This steak can be tough and needs to marinate. My advice is to marinate it over night.

Ingredients

Flank steak; calculate about 3 ounces per guest

Fresh mango, peeled and sliced 1/8 inch thick; calculate a couple of slices

per person

Olive oil

Balsamic vinegar

Balsamic Vinegar Marinade for the Steak:

Olive oil

Balsamic vinegar

Chopped garlic

Chopped parsley

Salt and pepper

Procedure

To prepare ½ cup of marinade, whisk together 2 cloves of chopped garlic, 1 ounce balsamic vinegar, 3 ounces olive oil, salt, and pepper.

Marinate the steak over night. Heat the grill.

Cook the steak for 3 to 5 minutes on each side. Let it rest for 5 minutes. While the steak is resting, brush the mango with olive oil and grill it for a minute on each side. The idea is to mark the fruit so that it caramelizes a bit but not to cook it through. Slice the steak along the grain as thin as possible. Cut the grilled mango into strips and arrange it with the steak. Garnish with parsley and a drizzle of balsamic vinegar.

Colorful Peppers, Tossed with Vidalia Onions, Garlic, Anchovies, and Olive Oil

We would call these "roasted" peppers but the process involves burning off the skin, peeling and then slicing the peppers. Some recipes call for baking the peppers (capsicums, or sweet peppers) in a hot oven until the skin turns black. I don't recommend this because the pepper cooks for so long that it becomes mush. Instead, we burn the skin by exposing the pepper to a hot fire for a short time and turning the pepper so that it burns evenly. Additionally, recipes for "roasted" peppers often instruct the cook to place the burned peppers in a paper bag after the fire treatment. The theory is that the skin will be more easily removed after steaming in a bag. This too I don't recommend because steaming the peppers cooks them too much, and because the skin will come off easily without the bag treatment.

In recent years, delicious greenhouse peppers in all sizes have reached the market and are always available. For roasting purposes I prefer the red, yellow, and orange bell peppers that are often packaged together. If Vidalia onions are not available, use another sweet onion.

Ingredients

Red, yellow, and orange bell peppers; calculate ½ pepper per person

Whole Vidalia onions, stems removed; calculate 1 per person

Chopped garlic

Olive oil

Red wine vinegar

Parsley

Salt and pepper

Anchovies (optional)

Procedure

Prepare a hot fire. Torch the peppers without cutting or trimming them. Turn them so that they blacken evenly. This will take about 5 minutes. When they are black, set them aside to cool for a few minutes.

Grill the onions. If using a large onion, slice it about ¼ inch thick and grill the slices. If using smaller Vidalias, cut them in half and grill the bulbs.

When the peppers are cool, drizzle cold water over them and peel the burned skin with your hands. Take away the core. Wash and dry the cleaned peppers. Slice them into strips. Add the grilled onions. Toss with garlic and olive oil. Finish with anchovies if you wish. Arrange the mixture on a platter. Sprinkle parsley, a splash of vinegar, and extra olive oil as necessary. Garnish with more parsley.

Skewer It

The remainder of this chapter is devoted to grilling foods on skewers, which is fun and the results are perfect for festive group-dining occasions. One can purchase wooden skewers in various sizes; these must always be soaked before being exposed to hot grill fires. Metal skewers, sometimes quite fancy, are also available and can be used over and over again.

There are a few general points to make about this manner of preparation. First, I recommend combining three ingredients that work together and look good, usually two of each alternated on the skewer. Second, the ingredients on the skewer should be about the same size. Third, the ingredients on the skewer should all be cooked properly in the same amount of time, usually about five to eight minutes. This means that sometimes you have to give one or another ingredient a head start before grilling, as indicated below. Fourth, feel free to select your own combinations of ingredients. Those shown below are some of our favorites.

Sausage, Mini Peppers, and Vidalia Onions on Skewers

You can use pork sausage, chicken, turkey, lamb, or any other sausage. Many supermarkets now sell already cooked chicken and turkey sausage. If you use these products, there's no need to cook them before grilling.

Ingredients

Sausage links; calculate 2 pieces of sausage about 1 inch in length for each skewer

Mini peppers; calculate 2 peppers for each skewer

Vidalia or other sweet onions

Olive oil

Salt and pepper

Procedure

Heat the grill. I recommend cooking the sausage in a 350 degree oven for 15 minutes before you grill it. The onions and peppers don't need to cook as long as the sausage and will be overcooked if grilled alongside raw sausage. Already cooked chicken and turkey sausage do not need to be cooked before grilling.

After the sausage as been partially cooked, cut it into 1 inch pieces and skewer it.

Place whole peppers on the skewer, alternating with other ingredients. Slide a couple of small whole onions on the skewer or slice larger onions and affix them to the skewer. Each item on the skewer should be about the same size. Brush the vegetables with olive oil, and grill the skewers for 5 to 7 minutes, until the onions and peppers are burned a bit and the sausage is heated through. Arrange on platters and serve, hot, or warm – but not cold.

Chicken Tenders with Radicchio and Onion on Skewers

Ingredients

Chicken Tenderloins, cut so that they are about 1 inch long; calculate 2 pieces per skewer

Radicchio, 6 chunks of radicchio from each head

Sweet onions

Olive oil

Ground fennel seeds

Salt and pepper

Procedure

Heat the grill. Season the chicken with salt, pepper, and ground fennel.

Cut the radicchio into wedges that can be secured to the skewer. Use small onions whole or cut larger onions so that they can be secured to the skewer. Arrange the skewers with alternating ingredients, 2 pieces of each. Brush with olive oil and grill for 5 to 8 minutes, turning frequently. Arrange on a platter and serve, hot to room temperature.

Large Scallops with Crimini Mushrooms and Artichokes on Skewers

For this recipe I recommend the commercially packaged artichokes rather than fresh artichokes. The fresh variety is more difficult to handle because of the tough outer leaves. You will need the liquid from the packaged artichokes for marinating the scallops.

Ingredients

Scallops, under 10 to the pound,
2 per skewer

Crimini mushrooms, left whole,

2 per skewer

Marinated artichokes; save the juice

Chopped parsley

Procedure

Heat the grill. Marinate the scallops using the liquid in which the artichokes are packed. Let stand at least 1 hour. Arrange ingredients on a skewer, alternating them: 1 scallop, 1 mushroom, 1 artichoke, and then repeat.

Grill for 7 minutes, turning frequently to avoid uneven cooking. The scallops should be cooked medium rare, about 140 degrees internal temperature, moist and delicious. Arrange on platters and serve, hot or at room temperature.

PORK TENDERLOIN WITH SQUID TENTACLES AND PLUM TOMATOES ON SKEWERS

Both pork and squid need to marinate for at least an hour. Squid tentacles can be purchased at Asian food stores. If purchased frozen, squid will need to marinate for a longer period of time.

INGREDIENTS

Pork tenderloin, cut into meaty morsels about 1 inch long

Squid tentacles

Roma tomatoes

FOR THE MARINADE:

Olive oil

Lemon juice

Dried oregano

Chopped parsley

Salt and pepper

PROCEDURE

To make a simple marinade for the pork and squid, whisk together lemon juice and olive oil (1 teaspoon lemon juice for each 4 tablespoons olive oil), finely diced garlic, oregano, salt and pepper to taste, and chopped parsley.

Marinate the pork for at least 1 hour.

Marinate the squid separately, but in the same marinade for an hour. If the squid is frozen, let it thaw in the marinade and give it an extra hour.

Heat the grill. The pork needs a head start: grill it for 5 minutes before putting it on skewers. This can be done well in advance.

Cut the tomatoes in half, lengthwise. Season the tomatoes with salt and dried oregano. Assemble the skewer with alternating ingredients: pork, squid, tomato, repeat. Grill the skewer for about 6 minutes, turning to ensure even cooking. Arrange on a platter and serve, hot or warm, but not cold.

Shrimp with Fennel and Oranges on Skewers

The shrimp will have to marinate for an hour or more.

Ingredients

Shrimp, under 15 to the pound, calculate 2 shrimp per skewer

Fennel, yielding 6 chunks of fennel

per head; calculate 2 chunks per skewer

Oranges

For the Marinade:

Orange juice

Olive oil

Garlic

Mint

Salt and pepper

Parsley

Procedure

To make the marinade, whisk together orange juice and olive oil (1 tablespoon orange juice for 3 tablespoons olive oil) along with finely chopped garlic, salt, pepper, and chopped mint.

Marinate the shrimp for about 1 hour or more in the refrigerator.

Cut the fennel into wedges that will be placed on the skewer, about the same size as the shrimp. Cut the oranges into wedges, leaving the skin on. Arrange the ingredients on skewers, alternating shrimp, fennel and orange wedges. Leave space so that everything is exposed to the fire.

Heat the grill. Grill the skewers until the shrimp is cooked through, about 5 minutes, turning to ensure even cooking. Arrange skewers on an attractive platter with additional orange slices.

Ode to Zucchini Blossoms and Honest Weight

In Italy and Spain one sees zucchini blossoms in many vegetable markets. At home they are hard to find. One summer I asked Gayle Anderson –vegetable, fruit, and plants guru at the Honest Weight Food Co-op—if she knew of any farmers who might bring me zucchini blossoms. Gayle inquired and found one Hudson Valley farmer named Migliori who was as excited to bring me zucchini flowers as I was to receive them. He could never sell them, he told Gayle, and so most of them rotted away – a culinary pity of extreme proportions.

In the growing season, I use the Honest Weight Food Co-op as a medium between Café Capriccio and local farmers. Instead of dealing directly with the myriad of local farms in the Hudson Valley, I work with the Co-op, receiving a list each week of products available from local farms.

The Co-op also offers copious selections of cheese, specialty oils (including black and white truffle oils and the most exquisite olive oils), olives, and other gourmet foods gathered together by the incomparable Gustav Ericson, one of Albany's most valuable culinary assets. Gustav's brilliant marketing technique is to offer all customers samples of everything, which they then cannot resist hoarding for themselves. In this way he keeps his customers deliriously happy and his business reasonably solvent.

The Co-op also sells a wide variety of organic foods, including free range meats from local farms, and eggs from chickens who are allowed to hunt and peck for food. The difference between mass produced eggs and those produced by liberated chickens is enormous: the shells are harder, the yolks are brighter, and the taste is exponentially better. I remember serving an antipasto-style lunch which I had carefully prepared for my discerning friend Mr. Anthony Verdoni, a wine importer, connoisseur of food, wine, and opera. The meal included hard-boiled eggs from the Co-op. I had also made several small dishes which constituted the lunch we shared. At the end he expressed satisfaction, and then asked: "where did those eggs come from?" They were the most memorable part of lunch — a couple of hard boiled eggs.

Returning to the subject of zucchini blossoms: they are the flowers of the male plant and are extremely delicate, with a shelf life of a couple of days. The Italians prepare them in many ways, usually deep fried. Last year I had a chance to prepare them often and decided that the best recipes for them are the three that follow.

Zucchini Blossoms Stuffed with Goat Cheese and Herbs

These are irresistible; calculate about 3 per guest.

Ingredients

Fresh zucchini blossoms

Soft goat cheese, about 1 teaspoon
for each blossom

Lemon wedges for garnish

Beaten eggs

Sifted flour

Olive oil for frying (deep fry)

Procedure

Open the flower and remove the pistils from inside. If you see a bug, remove that
too. Do not clean the flowers by washing them. Take a chance; blow them clean if
you must, but they are too delicate to wash.

Stuff each flower with a teaspoon of goat cheese. Lightly dust each flower with
flour. Dip each flower in the beaten eggs. Deep fry them for about 2 minutes.
Transfer the fried flowers to a paper towel. Arrange on a platter, garnished with
lemon wedges.

Frittata with Zucchini Blossoms Stuffed with Ricotta and Basil

A pastry bag is useful for stuffing the blossoms with the ricotta cheese mixture.

Ingredients – for a frittata to serve 8

10 zucchini Blossoms

8 ounces ricotta cheese

10 large free range eggs

½ cup chopped basil

Salt and pepper

3 tablespoons butter

1 tablespoon olive oil

Procedure

Mix the ricotta with 1 beaten egg, ¼ cup chopped basil, salt, and pepper.

Transfer contents to a pastry bag. Open the flower and remove the pistils.

Stuff each flower with ricotta using the pastry bag. Scramble the eggs in a bowl. Add remaining basil, salt and pepper. Gently transfer the stuffed zucchini blossoms to the bowl with eggs. Heat the butter and olive in a non stick omelet pan. Add the eggs and blossoms, being sure to distribute the blossoms evenly. Cook the frittata for several minutes. Without turning the frittata, place it in the oven for about 15 minutes at 400° F, until it is cooked through. Turn on to a plate and serve warm.

Zucchini Blossoms Stuffed with Mascarpone, Fresh Tomato Salsa

Calculate 2 to 3 blossoms for each guest. A pastry bag will help for stuffing the blossoms.

Ingredients

24 zucchini blossoms

24 ounces mascarpone cheese

For the Salsa:

3 cups cherry tomatoes, halved

1 sweet onion, chopped

½ cup celery hearts, chopped

Chopped parsley

Juice from 2 fresh limes

Olive oil

Salt and pepper

Procedure

Add 5 tablespoons fresh parsley to the mascarpone. Mix together and transfer to a pastry bag. Open the flower and remove the pistils. Stuff each flower with mascarpone using the pastry bag. Chill the stuffed blossoms for about 20 minutes.

To make the salsa, add tomatoes to the chopped sweet onion and celery. Toss with lime juice and olive oil, 4 parts oil to 1 part juice. Season with salt and pepper, and finish with parsley.

Arrange the stuffed blossoms on a platter surrounded with fresh tomato salsa.

STUFF IT

The venerable 1950 Gourmet Cookbook (1950: Gourmet Distributing Corporation) describes stuffing as "the most eminent of edible garnishes," and offers three sound principles for cooks like ourselves: let the stuffing cool before filling what is to be stuffed; allow for expansion during cooking by filling loosely; and, in the matter of a stuffed bird, let it rest over night before cooking in order to "mellow" it.

Stuffing is less a cooking technique than it is a method for creating a dish with a culinary personality perhaps more interesting than the parts themselves. Long sweet peppers grilled or roasted are always good, but peppers stuffed with savory sausage can be sublime. Notice that stuffed foods often combine meats, fish, cheese, vegetables, bread, and other food products together, sometimes in surprising ways. For example, I like to include pork with shellfish, as in the recipe for clams with prosciutto. Pasta can be stuffed with meat, fish, rice or vegetables to produce colorful and delicious dishes. And some combinations seem to be born for each other: eggplant and lamb, for example. The versatility of stuffed foods is reflected in the recipes that follow, which include delectable stuffings for meat, fish, pasta, and vegetables. Our Chef's Table dinners always include at least one stuffed preparation such as those that follow.

Sweet Peppers Stuffed with Pork and Spices

My favorite peppers for stuffing are long, red, and sweet. They are greenhouse grown by the Sunset Company and named Ancient Peppers. Any pepper you like will do for stuffing; small bell peppers can be stuffed whole, while larger ones can be cut in half or quarters. For this recipe we will stuff my favorites.

Ingredients

Red peppers, long and sweet; 6 to 8 inches long, approximately 1 to 1 ½ inches in diameter; calculate 1 pepper for 2 diners

Ingredients for Stuffing (2 ounces for each pepper):

1 pound ground pork (use other ground meats if you prefer, such as lamb, chicken, or veal)

1 cup breadcrumbs

2 whole eggs

½ cup grated Pecorino Romano

½ cup chopped parsley

1 teaspoon grated fennel seeds

Chopped garlic to your taste

Salt and pepper

Procedure

Trim the tops off the peppers. Remove the cores and cut the peppers in half, diagonally. This will give you 2 peppers about 3 to 4 inches long with the circumference flesh completely intact.

To make the stuffing, mix all stuffing ingredients together and let rest for an hour at room temperature. Stuff each pepper with about 2 ounces of meat mixture. Bake at 400 degrees for 20 to 25 minutes. The meat should be at 160 degrees internal temperature. Arrange the peppers on a platter and serve hot, warm, or at room temperature.

Asian Eggplant Stuffed with Spicy Lamb

Ingredients

Eggplant, 1 inch or more in diameter

Lamb Stuffing (2 ounces for each piece of stuffed eggplant):

1 pound ground lamb

1 cup breadcrumbs

2 whole eggs

½ cup chopped parsley

½ teaspoon grated cloves

½ teaspoon grated allspice

¼ teaspoon grated cinnamon

¼ teaspoon hot pepper (Utica Grind)

Chopped garlic to your taste

Salt and pepper

Procedure

Cut the eggplant in half lengthwise. Dig a trench in the center, about ¼ inch deep and ½ inch or more in width if possible. Cut the prepared eggplant into 3-inch long pieces.

To make the stuffing, mix stuffing ingredients together and let rest for 1 hour at room temperature. Stuff the eggplant strips. Bake them for about 20 minutes at 400 degrees. Arrange on a platter and serve hot, warm, or at room temperature.

Portobello Mushrooms Stuffed with Sausage

Ingredients

Whole portobello mushrooms, stems removed; calculate 1 mushroom (cut into halves) for each diner

Sausage for stuffing; calculate 2 to 3 ounces of stuffing for each mushroom, depending on its size

Procedure

Clean the mushrooms and trim the stems. Stems can be chopped and added to the sausage. Select your favorite sausage – pork, chicken, turkey, or lamb – and remove it from its casing. Add chopped mushroom stems to the sausage if you wish. Stuff each mushroom with 2 to 3 ounces of the mix, depending on the size of the mushroom.

Bake them whole for 20 minutes at 400 degrees. Cut the mushrooms in half and arrange on a platter garnished with *radicchio rosso*. Serve hot or warm.

Zucchini with Mushrooms, Bread, and Mozzarella Stuffing

Ingredients

Fresh zucchini, about 8 inches long; calculate 1 zucchini for every 2 guests

Mushroom Stuffing (about 2 ounces of stuffing for each zucchini):

1 pound mushrooms, cleaned and chopped

1 cup fine breadcrumbs

3 whole eggs

1 cup grated mozzarella cheese

¼ cup Pecorino Romano

Chopped parsley

Salt and pepper

Procedure

Cut the zucchini in half lengthwise and then again on the diagonal. This will give you 4 pieces of zucchini, each about 4 inches long.

Make a small trench in the center of each piece of zucchini to hold the stuffing.

To prepare the stuffing (approximately 24 ounces), mix everything together and let stand for an hour. Stuff the zucchini and bake for about 25 minutes at 400° F. The stuffing should be golden on top and the zucchini still firm. Arrange on platters and serve hot or warm.

CALAMARI TUBES STUFFED WITH SEAFOOD RICE

Calculate 1 per guest with a few extra.

INGREDIENTS: FOR 16 SQUID

16 calamari tubes, about 3 inches in length

Seafood rice (approximately 32 ounces, sufficient to stuff 16 squid):

2 cups long grain rice

16 ounces mixed seafood of choice (chopped into small pieces) such as squid tentacles, bay scallops, canned tuna, chopped clams, or white fish—choose your own combinations

4 cups of water

1 medium onion, chopped

Lemons

1/8 teaspoon saffron

1 can anchovies (2 ounces)

1 teaspoon capers

Chopped parsley

toothpicks

PROCEDURE

For the stuffing, sauté onion in olive oil for several minutes, until the onion takes on some color. Add the seafood and anchovies; continue cooking for a couple of minutes. Add the rice and stir everything together, continuing to sauté for 2 more minutes. Add water to the mixture, along with saffron and parsley. Cover and let the rice cook for about 15 minutes.

Stuff each squid with 2 ounces of stuffing. Secure by sealing the squid tube with a toothpick. Bake the stuffed squid, covered, at 400 degrees for 20 minutes.

Arrange on a platter garnished with lemon wedges and fresh parsley.

Calamari Tubes Stuffed with Pork Sausage, Baked with Tomatoes

Ingredients for 16 squid

16 Calamari tubes, about 3 inches long; calculate 1 per diner with a few extra

2 pounds Italian-style pork sausage; calculate 2 ounces to stuff each calamari tube

1 can Italian plum tomatoes (28 ounces)

2 cloves garlic, chopped

2 tablespoons olive oil

Basil chopped

Parsley, chopped

Pinch of hot pepper (Utica Grind)

Procedure

For the sauce, sauté garlic in olive oil for 1 minute. Add the tomatoes, hot pepper, and fresh basil. Simmer for 10 minutes.

For the stuffing, remove sausage from its casing. Stuff each squid tube with 2 ounces of sausage. Secure the stuffing with a toothpick inserted into the top of the tube.

Arrange squid in a pan and evenly distribute half of the sauce over it. Cover and bake for 30 minutes. Let it rest for a few minutes, then arrange the squid on a platter, top with extra sauce, garnish with fresh basil and parsley.

Clams, Stuffed and Baked, with Prosciutto

This recipe calls for 12 clams, which will yield 24 stuffed clams, since each of the clam's 2 shells will be stuffed. Calculate 2 stuffed clams for each guest. One of these delicious morsels will not be enough. Use littleneck or cherrystone clams. Cherrystone clams are larger and will yield more substance.

Ingredients

12 clams

6 cloves chopped garlic

1 cup Italian plum tomatoes

2 cups fine breadcrumbs

1 tablespoon dried oregano

1 tablespoon capers

2 ounces anchovies, chopped

3 ounces prosciutto chopped

Chopped parsley

Procedure

Open the clams, sift the liquid through a strainer, and set it aside. Chop the clams and place them into a bowl. Add the tomatoes, along with garlic, oregano, capers, anchovies, prosciutto, and parsley. Mix all ingredients together. Add the bread crumbs and the clam liquid. Mix together; the mixture should be moist but not swimming. Stuff 24 clam shells with the stuffing. Bake uncovered until crispy, about 15 minutes.

Arrange on platters and serve hot or warm.

Chicken Thighs Stuffed with Spicy Chicken

Each thigh will get 2 ounces of stuffing.

Ingredients (for 12 guests)

12 chicken thighs, boneless; calculate 1 thigh for each diner

For the Stuffing:

1½ pounds ground chicken

1 tablespoon ground fennel

4 cloves minced garlic

¼ teaspoon hot pepper (Utica Grind) flakes

½ cup fine breadcrumbs

3 ounces grated Pecorino Romano

2 whole eggs

Chopped parsley

Salt and pepper

Toothpicks

Procedure

For the stuffing, combine the ground chicken with all ingredients listed above. Mix well and let the mixture rest in the refrigerator for at least an hour.

Remove the skin from each thigh. Pound each thigh on the inside to increase its surface by about 20 percent and to even it a bit. Place 2 ounces of stuffing in the center of each thigh.

Wrap the thigh around the stuffing and secure it with 1 or 2 toothpicks. Bake the thighs in the oven at 400 degrees for 25 minutes. Let the cooked thighs rest for 10 minutes. Slice them a half-inch thick, arrange on a platter attractively garnished, and serve warm or at room temperature.

Pork Tenderloin Stuffed with Pork and Quail Eggs

Pork tenderloins vary somewhat in size. For this recipe we will assume that the tenderloins you select are about 10 inches long and weigh approximately 1 pound. They will yield 12 to 14 slices for your platter; calculate 2 slices per diner. Quail eggs are used in this recipe because they are less than 1 inch long and will nicely into the stuffed port roll.

Ingredients

1 pork tenderloin, approximately 10 inches long, weighing 1 pound

10 quail eggs

For the Stuffing:

8 ounces ground pork

2 ounces fine bread crumbs

2 cloves minced garlic

1 egg

1/8 teaspoon ground fennel seeds

Chopped parsley

Salt and pepper

toothpicks

Procedure

For the stuffing, mix the stuffing ingredients and let rest for at least an hour.

Boil the quail eggs for 7 minutes. Cool them in cold water, then peel away the shells. Butterfly the pork tenderloin by slicing it longitudinally and opening it. With a meat bat, pound the tenderloin to spread it further and smooth its surface. Arrange the stuffing in the center of the tenderloin, from top to bottom. Press the peeled quail eggs into the stuffing consecutively from top to bottom. Wrap the tenderloin around the stuffing and secure it with toothpicks. Roast the tenderloin for about 25 minutes at 400 degrees. Let it rest for at least 15 minutes. Slice the tenderloin in half-inch pieces, arrange on a platter, and garnish with something colorful. No need for a sauce. Serve warm or at room temperature.

Beef Braciola Simmered in Tomato Sauce

Ingredients

Beef cube steak, each piece weighing about 4 ounces; calculate 1 piece for each guest

1 slice of prosciutto for each braciola

2 tablespoons breadcrumbs for each braciola, seasoned with Pecorino

Romano and chopped parsley

Italian plum tomatoes

Chopped garlic

Olive oil

Procedure

Lightly pound the cube steak to reduce its width and expand its surface.

For 1 ¼ cups of seasoned breadcrumbs, mix 8 ounces of fine breadcrumbs with ¼ cup grated Pecorino Romano and plenty of chopped parsley.

Place a slice of prosciutto along the surface of the meat. Sprinkle the seasoned bread crumbs over the prosciutto. Roll the meat around the stuffing and secure with string or toothpicks. Brown the meat in little olive oil, approximately 3 minutes. Add chopped garlic for 30 seconds – never burn the garlic. Add plum tomatoes to cover the meat. Simmer for 20 minutes. Let the meat rest for at least 10 minutes in the sauce. To serve, slice the meat into 3 pieces and arrange on a platter.

Serve the sauce on the side or place a dollop on each slice of meat.

Tubular Pasta (Paccheri) Stuffed with Sausage and Baked with Tomato Sauce

When I was a boy, my mother's special birthday supper for me included rigatoni, stuffed with sausage and baked with tomato sauce. For this recipe we will be using *paccheri*, which is twice as big as rigatoni and easier to stuff. *Paccheri* is a very large tubular pasta found in the cuisine of Naples. The package of *paccheri* I have before me weighs 500 grams (slightly more than 1 pound), and it contains about 50 tubes.

Ingredients

1 pound of *paccheri*

1 ounce of Italian style pork sausage uncooked
and out of its casing for each pasta tube

For the Sauce:

2 cans Italian plum tomatoes
(each 28 ounces), to make sauce
for 1 pound of pasta

Olive oil

5 cloves minced garlic

Fresh basil

Chopped parsley

Pinch of hot pepper (Utica Grind)

Salt and pepper

Procedure

To make the sauce, sauté garlic in olive oil for a minute. Add tomatoes, basil, parsley, salt, and both peppers. Simmer the sauce for 10 minutes.

Boil the *paccheri* in salted water for 5 minutes. This will soften them and facilitate stuffing. After 5 minutes, plunge the pasta into a cool water bath. Ladle some sauce into the bottom of a casserole. Stuff each tube with about 1 ounce of pork sausage and arrange in the casserole. Spoon some sauce on top of the first layer of pasta. Continue stuffing and layering the pasta in the casserole, topping each layer with sauce, including the top layer. When the pasta is stuffed and organized in the casserole, cover and bake for 30 minutes at 400 degrees. Let it rest for 15 minutes. Serve it from the casserole with sauce on the side.

Colossal Pasta Shells Stuffed with Ricotta and Baked with Tomato Sauce

This is a variation on the recipe above, but with a meatless filling for the pasta.

Ingredients

1 pound of colossal pasta shells (about 50 shells to a pound); calculate 2 shells per person

Ricotta filling:

Ricotta cheese; calculate 1 ounce per shell

2 whole eggs for 1 pound of ricotta

Chopped parsley

For the Sauce:

2 cans Italian plum tomatoes (each 28 ounces), to make sauce for 1 pound of pasta

Olive oil

5 cloves minced garlic

Fresh basil

Chopped parsley

Pinch of hot pepper (Utica Grind)

Salt and pepper

Procedure

For the ricotta filling, combine 1 pound of ricotta with 2 whole eggs, ¼ teaspoon of salt, and plenty of parsley. Mix well.

For the sauce, sauté garlic in olive oil for a minute. Add tomatoes, basil, parsley, salt, pepper, and hot pepper. Simmer the sauce for 10 minutes.

Boil the shells in salted water for 5 minutes. This will soften them and facilitate stuffing. After 5 minutes, plunge the pasta into a cool water bath. Ladle some sauce in the bottom of the casserole. Stuff each tube with about one ounce of ricotta and arrange in the casserole. Spoon some sauce on top of the first layer of pasta. Continue stuffing and layering the pasta in the casserole, topping each layer with sauce, including the top layer. When the pasta is stuffed and organized in the casserole, cover and bake it for 30 minutes at 400 degrees. Let it rest for half an hour. Serve it from the casserole with sauce on the side.

Braise It

B raising is a technique of cooking meat with heat generated by liquid. In my approach, this usually means wine combined with aromatic vegetables (root vegetables, leeks, onions, shallots, garlic), herbs, broths, marinades, or sometimes plain water. Braising occurs in the oven or on top of the stove. If you braise on the stove, you must attentively control heat and stir as necessary. If you braise in the oven, you can usually walk away from your project for a couple of hours. I like to braise foods in terra cotta pots called *tiella* in Italian and *cazuela* in Spanish. Terra cotta distributes heat in a special way that provides a perfect braising environment. Terra cotta also holds heat for a long time and the *tiella* is an impressive sight on your chef's table.

Braising is good for cooking meat that would otherwise be tough. Braised foods in this book are cooked for at least one and one half hours. The Italians call this *stracotto,* which translates to something like "cooked extra," i.e., cooked for a long time.

Braising begins by browning the meat and then introducing the liquid that will become sauce for the finished dish. That initial browning followed by long cooking in the flavorful liquid distinguishes braising from poaching and boiling. Meats in these recipes will be browned in several ways: on a grill, in the oven, in the pan, and sometimes on the stovetop grill, the *gratella.* Braised meats are always cooked covered, and rather slowly.

The magic of braising is that lesser cuts of meat – thrifty cuts, if you will – emerge succulent and redolent of exotic flavors and textures. And braised dishes are always best when prepared the day before, allowed to cool thoroughly, fat removed, then reheated and served.

I always approach braising as a four-step process:

1. Create the braising liquid on top of the stove by browning the vegetables, sometimes adding thickening agents, then liquids and herbs. Simmer for a few minutes.

2. Brown the meat while the liquids are simmering. Whenever possible, I use the oven. At high temperature, the oven gives meat a crisp and (most importantly) flavorful exterior that permeates the dish. It is also clean and effortless.

3. Ladle the liquid and vegetables over the meat when it is browned and the braising potion is ready. Be sure to distribute the solids evenly in the pot. Cover the preparation and put into the oven until done.

4. Let the finished dish rest for at least thirty minutes. After that time, skim the fat from the top and then prepare the sauce in ways described.

Braised Short Ribs of Beef

Select ribs that are about 2 inches thick. Sizes will vary. Calculate 1 or 2 ribs per person depending on the size of the ribs.

Ingredients for 8 Servings

5 pounds short ribs

2 onions, chopped

½ cup diced carrots

½ cup diced celery

4 garlic cloves

3 bay leaves

1 tablespoon rosemary

½ cup flour

4 tablespoons olive oil

1 bottle red wine (750 ml.)

1 small can of tomato paste (6 ounces)

1 cup water

Salt and pepper

Procedure

Season the ribs with salt and pepper. Brown them in the oven at 500º F for 20 minutes. Sauté onions in olive oil until they take on some color, approximately 5 minutes. Add carrots, celery and garlic and sauté for several minutes. Add flour, tomato paste, and 1 cup of wine. Stir until smooth, about 2 minutes. Add the remaining ingredients. Simmer for about 10 minutes.

When the meat is browned, add the braising potion to the meat, cover with foil and place in the oven at 325 degrees for 2 ½ hours. When finished, let rest for 30 minutes, skim the fat, and then reduce the liquid to create a rich sauce. Serve from a platter or, if you prepared the ribs in terra cotta, serve from that. Garnish with sauce on top, parsley and sauce on the side.

Top Blade Steak Braised (Stracotto di Manzo)

Top blade steak is part of the chuck. They have a gelatinous quality when finished that melts in the mouth. Steaks should be ¾ inch thick. Calculate 1 per person with a few extra. Each steak will weigh about 4 ounces.

Ingredients for 8 servings

Top blade steaks, calculate 1 per person with a few extra

2 onions, chopped

½ cup diced leeks

½ cup diced celery

4 garlic cloves

3 bay leaves

½ teaspoon fresh rosemary

½ cup flour

4 tablespoons olive oil

1 bottle red wine (750 ml.)

1 small can of tomato paste (6 ounces)

1 cup water

Salt and pepper

Procedure

Season the steaks with salt and pepper. Brown them over a grill or on top of the stove. Lay them in a baking dish in 1 or 2 layers.

Sauté onions in olive oil until they take on some color, approximately 5 minutes. Add carrots, leeks and garlic and sauté for several minutes. Add flour, tomato paste, and one cup of wine. Stir until smooth, about 2 minutes. Add the remaining ingredients. Simmer for about 10 minutes.

When the meat is browned, add the braising potion to the meat, cover with foil and place in the oven at 325 degrees for 2 hours. Let rest for 30 minutes, skim the fat, and then reduce the liquid to create a rich sauce. Arrange steaks on a platter, with sauce on top and some on the side.

BRAISED OXTAIL

Oxtails are usually packaged already cut.

INGREDIENTS FOR 8 SERVINGS

8 pounds oxtails, cut at the joints

2 large onions, chopped

1 cup chopped carrots

6 garlic cloves

4 bay leaves

1 small can tomato paste (6 ounces)

1 bottle red wine (750 ml.)

½ cup flour

Olive oil

Salt and pepper to taste

Parsley for garnish

PROCEDURE

Season the oxtails with salt and pepper then grill them for a few minutes on each side. This will render some fat and give them a crispy texture.

To create the braising potion, sauté onions in olive oil until they take on some color, approximately 5 minutes. Add carrots and garlic and sauté for several minutes. Add flour, tomato paste, and 1 cup of wine. Stir until smooth, about 2 minutes. Add the remaining ingredients. Simmer for about 10 minutes.

When the meat is browned, add the braising potion to the meat, cover with foil, and place into the oven at 325 degrees for 3 hours. Let rest for a half hour, skim the fat, and then reduce the liquid to create a rich sauce. Serve from a platter or, if you prepared the oxtails in terra cotta, serve from that. Finish with parsley and sauce.

Braised Pork Hocks (Ossobuco di Maiale)

This is an adaptation of the ossobuco recipe we use at the Café Capriccio to prepare veal shanks and lamb shanks.

Ingredients for 8 Servings

8 pork hocks, 1½ inches thick

1 cup chopped onion

½ cup chopped celery

½ cup chopped carrots

4 cloves garlic

1 tablespoon chopped rosemary

½ tablespoon sage

3 bay leaves

1 can San Marzano tomatoes (28 ounces)

2 cups dry white wine

Salt and pepper

Chopped parsley

Procedure

Brown the pork hocks. Sauté onions in olive oil until they take on some color, approximately 5 minutes. Add carrots, celery, and garlic and sauté for several minutes. Add the remaining ingredients. Simmer for about 10 minutes.

When the meat is browned, add the braising potion to the meat, cover with foil, and place into the oven at 325 degrees for 2 hours. Let rest for 30 minutes, skim the fat, and then reduce the liquid to create a rich sauce. Serve from a platter or, if you prepared the ribs in terra cotta, serve from that with sauce on top and more sauce on the side.

Chicken Cacciatore

For the chicken, select 2 chickens, 3 to 3 ½ pounds, each cut into serving pieces. Or you can buy breasts, legs, and thighs already cut and packaged. Cut the breasts in half so that pieces are uniform in size. Calculate on 2 pieces of chicken per guest.

Ingredients for 8 Servings

2 pieces of chicken per guest

5 portobello mushrooms, sliced

1 cup chopped onion

1 cup chopped sweet red pepper

6 cloves garlic

¼ teaspoon hot pepper (Utica Grind)

1 can San Marzano tomatoes (28 ounces)

1 tablespoon dried oregano

3 bay leaves

Salt and pepper

Chopped parsley

Procedure

Season the chicken with salt, pepper, and oregano. Brown the pieces by sautéing in olive oil for 5 minutes.

In a separate skillet, sauté onions in olive oil until they take on color, approximately 5 minutes. Add peppers and continue cooking for several minutes. Add mushrooms and garlic and sauté for several minutes. Add the remaining ingredients. Simmer for about 10 minutes.

When the meat is browned, add the braising potion to the meat, cover with foil and place into the oven at 325 degrees for 45 minutes. Let rest for 30 minutes, skim the fat, then reduce the liquid to create a rich sauce. Arrange chicken on a platter garnished with vegetables and plenty of parsley; sauce on top and more on the side.

Lamb Stew (Spezzatina di Montone)

3 pounds boneless lamb stew, from the leg or shoulder (I prefer the shoulder)

1 cup chopped onion

½ cup chopped celery

½ cup chopped carrots

4 cloves garlic

1 tablespoon chopped rosemary

½ tablespoon sage

3 bay leaves

1 can San Marzano tomatoes (28 ounces)

2 cups dry white wine

Salt and pepper

Chopped parsley

Procedure

Season the lamb with rosemary, sage, salt, and pepper. Brown it on top of the stove by sautéing in olive oil for about 5 minutes.

In a separate skillet, sauté onions in olive oil until they take on some color, approximately 5 minutes. Add carrots, celery, and garlic and sauté for several minutes. Add the remaining ingredients. Simmer for about 10 minutes.

When the meat is browned, add the braising potion to the meat, cover with foil, and place into the oven at 325 degrees for 2 hours. Let rest for 30 minutes, skim the fat, and then reduce the liquid to create a rich sauce.

Stews are best served in an attractive, wide bowl. As always, finish with sauce on top and parsley and sauce on the side.

Braised Rabbit (Coniglio Ischitana)

Ischia is one of three beautiful islands in the Bay of Naples. There one finds the cuisine of nearby Naples, but the Ischitanae are particularly noted for pasta *puttanesca* and rabbit dishes. (The island is loaded with rabbits.) The domestic rabbits we buy in specialty stores (Asian markets, for example) have a wonderfully delicate flavor and succulent texture. They do not taste like "game."

Ingredients for 8 servings

Two 3-pound rabbits cut into serving pieces (see below)

1 medium onion, chopped

6 cloves garlic

1 can San Marzano tomatoes (28 ounces)

1 cup dry white wine

Olive oil

Salt and pepper

Chopped parsley

Procedure

Keeping the leg and thigh together, cut the breast lengthwise and then in half vertically, and cut the front legs and shoulders so that you have 2 pieces. The front leg/shoulder pieces are the most tender part of the rabbit, although they do not have much meat on them.

Sauté the garlic in olive oil until it shows some color. Discard the garlic. Sauté the onions for several minutes. Season the rabbit with salt and pepper, and then brown it with the onions.

After the rabbit is browned, add tomatoes and other ingredients. Stir it together, cover and place into the oven at 325 degrees for 1 ½ hours. Let the finished dish rest for a half-hour. There should be not much fat. Arrange the rabbit on a platter garnished with sauce and parsley.

Veal Stew with Mushrooms (Spezzatina di Vitella)

Ingredients for 8 servings

3½ pounds boneless veal stew, from the leg or shoulder (I prefer the shoulder)

1 cup chopped onion

5 portobello mushrooms, sliced

4 cloves garlic

1 tablespoon chopped rosemary

½ tablespoon sage

3 bay leaves

1 can tomato paste (6 ounces)

1 bottle dry white wine, 750 ml.

Salt and pepper

Chopped parsley

Procedure

Season the veal with rosemary, sage, salt, and pepper. Brown it on top of the stove by sautéing in olive oil for about 5 minutes. In a separate skillet, sauté onions in olive oil until they take on some color, approximately 5 minutes.

Add mushrooms and garlic and sauté for several minutes. Add the remaining ingredients. Simmer for 10 minutes.

When the veal is browned, add the braising potion to the meat, cover with foil, place into the oven at 325 degrees for 1 ½ hours. Let rest for 30 minutes, skim the fat, and then reduce the liquid to create a rich sauce.

Stews are best served in an attractive, wide bowl generously garnished with parsley and finished with sauce. Include sauce on the side as well.

Ivo

Yves Longhi was born in Versailles, near Paris, in 1928, shortly before the Great Depression and more than decade before the Great War which was to ravage Europe, his homeland. His mother was French and his father Italian, from the Veneto region near Verona. Yves (hereinafter named Ivo as I now call him after his paternal ethnicity) grew up mostly in France but also spent time in Italy with his father's family. His grandfather was a chef in Verona, his maternal grandfather a blacksmith in France, his uncle a prosperous farmer with a couple hundred head of cattle in the Veneto.

Ivo's father was in the restaurant trade, working in Italy and France. As a young man Ivo worked in kitchens and dining rooms in France, Italy and England, and later on the French-line cruise ships. In the 1950s he emigrated from London, where he was working at the prestigious Savoy Hotel, to the United States. Ivo told me that he had worked with some Italians in Europe who made it possible for him to secure his first employment here shortly after his arrival. The job was at the Stork Club in Manhattan, one of the City's legendary nightclubs, then at the height of its popularity. Ivo bent his nose a little from right to left when he described his first employers.

In the late 1950s Ivo found his way to Hillsdale in the Catskills where he opened his first restaurant named *L'auberge des Fougers*, the Inn of the Ferns. Later, in 1960, he opened Albany's first classic French restaurant in the historic Hudson River Day Line ticket office on Broadway, adjacent to the imposing central administrative offices of the State University of New York. The restaurant carried its name from Hillsdale, *Lauberge des Fougers.*

Later in the 1960s he opened a bistro named L'Ecole in Stuyvesant Plaza on Fuller Road in Albany. L'Ecole was a high spirited and affordable hotspot with the menu written daily on a blackboard, generic French wines like St. Emillion sold by the glass for a couple of dollars, and a staff of pretty coeds from the nearby State University.

After many years Ivo left the area but decided in his mid-seventies to open still another restaurant, Il Tartine, in the city of brotherly love, Philadelphia, Pennsylvania. This restaurant was as successful as all of his others but was short lived because hip replacement surgery forced our hero into retirement – albeit not for long.

Following recovery from surgery, Ivo visted Albany and stopped by Café Capriccio to say hello. I reminded him that in 1997, before I opened the Cooking and Wine School, I had invited him to join me at the stove for the inaugural dinner in the new kitchen and dining room that I had recently created. We invited a dozen friends, and together Ivo and I served the first group ever to dine at the Cooking and Wine School, later the Cooking and Wine Society, and now the Chef's Table–subject of this volume.

I recall telling Ivo on that fateful day of his visit that my son Franco had recently graduated from college and had decided to join me at Café Capriccio. Franco, today master of Café Capriccio's kitchen, was in his early 20s and had recently completed his college degree in Greek and Roman studies.

As we were discussing our respective conditions and circumstances it dawned on me that Ivo, clearly in transition, might be available to spend some time in Albany and perhaps keep a special eye on the young Franco, a person with high regard for history and the people who made history. I proposed this to Ivo, telling him that if he were so disposed he could live in an apartment we had available at Café Capriccio. We would welcome him into our personal and professional family, and he could show us all a few tricks of the trade. He could give special attention to Franco, who would see him every day; he could be a *maestro della cucina* with over sixty years of experience in Europe and the United States, he would be in the family and available all the time, just doing what comes naturally.

Ivo said he'd do it and he did. Shortly thereafter, Ivo arrived at the apartment and has been with us ever since. Franco continues to mature and we are all assured that whatever today's restaurant-related challenges may be, Ivo has seen them a hundred times and has strong opinions concerning how to address them. He is restaurant history personified, the institutional memory, intrepid, ready to advise, to lead, to charge – damn those torpedoes of outrageous fortune, full steam ahead. That's Ivo's philosophy. If you'd like to meet him, come by the Chef's Table some time; Ivo's always around.

Roast It

Roasting is the technique of cooking with dry heat, usually in an oven. Historically, foods were roasted on spits in front of a fireplace, and today I often roast meats in a covered charcoal- or wood-fired grill, such as a Weber kettle. When using the covered grill, I roast most of the meat with indirect heat by placing it to the far side, away from the fire.

In small villages in Europe, as well as in some rural settings I've seen in Italy, one can find large communal wood-fired ovens still used by many locals to roast meat and to bake bread. There is, for example, a large outdoor oven located at Fattoria Lavacchio, a vineyard in Tuscany where we have been taking holiday groups for more than a decade. Whenever we are there, we plan a dinner cooked in the forno di legno — the outdoor wood fired oven, the size of a small cabin. My daughter Anita was recently married at Fattoria Lavacchio, and her wedding feast for twenty five family and friends included an enormous side of beef expertly roasted by Sergio, the master of the forno di legno. On other visits, we have enjoyed wild boar, chickens that roam the vineyard, deer, rabbit, and other meat roasted in the forno. Sometimes the oven is used to bake Tuscan-style pizza at temperatures exceeding 800° F.

Cooks continue to debate the question of roasting temperatures. Some say the long, slow technique (325° F) is ideal; some prefer hot ovens that are said to seal juices and provide a crisp outer surface while keeping the meat tender and juicy within. Others recommend starting with high heat to seal the juices, then lowering the heat for the duration of cooking time. Wood-fired ovens, such as the large communal ones mentioned above, are maintained at much higher temperatures than are household ovens. All of this leads me to say that the subject of appropriate heat levels for roasting is much like rocket science, i.e., complicated, but it's also akin to an art form and sometimes the best approach seems to emanate from instinctual rather than scientific source. The best temperature, in other words, depends.

My preference is to roast birds like fat chickens and capons at relatively high heat (450° F) so that they turn out crisp and deeply colored; the same applies with large roasts of beef and pork. A rack of lamb, on the other hand, might best be cooked for ten minutes at high heat and then for twenty minutes more at a lower heat. Recipes below will provide suggestions which home chefs are free, of course, to modify.

One classic technique of roasting is to raise the meat above the fats and liquids that accumulate in the roasting pan. For this, racks are available to elevate the roast. Raising the roast allows for the dry heat of the oven to circulate around it and cook the bottom in the same way as it cooks the top. Roasts that are cooked in a pan immersed in the fats and juices that surround them will be soggy on the bottom. Meat cooked this way can look and taste great, but it won't have the uniform crispness of a perfect roast.

Above all guides and assists, I rely most upon a meat thermometer to guide me in determining when the roast is done. For many years I have used a heat-sensing device that nobody else I know has. It is called a Food Thermicator II, manufactured by Merlin Manufacturing Company in Ohio. It's a cumbersome device that is shaped like an aardvark and hangs on the wall, but it has a thin probe that gives an instant temperature reading, up to 500° F, on a digital screen, telling the cook that whatever she is cooking is rare, medium, well done, or cooked to death. Unfortunately, this device is very expensive, although it would seem that technology exists to create something like it for an affordable price. The last time I bought one, it cost more than three hundred dollars. Marlin does not list the price on its website (marlinmfg.com). I once wrote them a letter saying that I have owned these devices for twenty-five years and do not know anybody else who has one. If they could be made affordable, say fifty dollars, every cook in the country would own one. My advice fell upon deaf ears and I remain the only person in my circle who uses the Thermicator II – except for the friends and family who have received them as gifts from me.

Old school cooks sneer at my use of the Thermicator II, but I can't see how else to tell when the internal temperature of a fat chicken is at an exactly right 160° F. Recipes that instruct cooks to let the roast cook for twenty minutes per pound are not taking into account the shape of the meat. If a whole pork loin of uniform circumference weighs twelve pounds and the cook follows directions to cook it for twenty minutes per pound, then the cook will roast the pork for 240 minutes (four hours). If the cook roasts only one half of the pork loin cut diagonally, maintaining the same circumference, thus reducing only the length, then he would cook six pounds of pork for only two hours. Which is correct? Cooks have to use their own judgment about roasting times based on weight and thickness of meat, but the only sure way to know when it's done to your taste is to measure it.

The temperatures at which meats are called rare, medium, and well done, along with the recommended safe internal temperatures, vary and often seem conflicting. For example, some recipes recommend cooking pork to 180 to 200 degrees in order to kill parasites, when science tells us that 160° F is adequate– and our observations tell us that pork (or chicken or turkey or lamb or anything) roasted to 180° F will usually be grey, tough, and tasteless. Lean meats, for example, do not look good or taste good if roasted to extremely high internal temperatures; fatty meats, on the other hand, can be succulent even if cooked to 200° F.

GENERAL RULES RELATED TO DEGREE OF DONENESS ARE FOR ME:

Chicken should be roasted to 160 degrees

Pork should be roasted to 160 degrees

Rare means from 120 to 125 degrees internal temperature

Medium beef, veal, lamb: 130 to 135 degrees internal temperature

Medium-well beef, veal, lamb: 140 degrees to 150 degrees internal temperature

Well-done beef, veal, lamb: 160 degrees or more internal temperature

Roasts should always be basted in the oven and they should stand for a while before they are carved – fifteen minutes for small roasts, like stuffed chicken and lamb rack, and up to thirty minutes for larger roasts, such as standing ribs and holiday turkeys. Fabulous roasted meats often define holiday dining and will always be welcome additions to your chef's table.

Arista di Maiale Fiorentina – Roast Pork Florentine

Ingredients – For 10 to 12 Guests

1 pork rib roast with bones, approximately 8 pounds; size will vary, of course

4 cloves garlic

¼ cup fresh rosemary, chopped

3 pounds potatoes

Olive oil

Salt and pepper

Procedure

Expose the bones by trimming them 2 inches from the top. Scrape away fat and skin from the bones. Cut the potatoes for roasting, season them with salt, pepper, and rosemary. Drizzle potatoes with olive oil. Score the meat and rub it with salt, pepper, and fresh sage. Insert slivers of garlic into the meat wherever you can.

Preheat the oven to 450 degrees. Place a rack for the pork in a roasting pan large enough to hold the pork and the potatoes. Place the pork on the rack.

Spread the potatoes around the pork. Roast the pork and the potatoes for about 1½ hours, until the pork is 160 degrees at the center. Baste the pork several times during the roasting process. Let the pork stand for 20 minutes before carving.

Check the potatoes to ensure that they are tender inside and crisp outside. Potatoes can be finished on top of the stove while the pork rests, or they can be left in the oven. Adjust the heat as necessary. Carve the roast and display it on a platter with potatoes all around.

STUFFED GOOSE

INGREDIENTS – FOR 8 TO 10 GUESTS

1 goose, 10 pounds or more

6 slices of bacon (to cover the goose while roasting)

2 pounds aromatic vegetables

to roast with the goose: onions, leeks, carrots, other roots, garlic, shallots, scallions, your choice–any combination

3 cups dry white wine

FOR THE STUFFING:

1 pound fennel sausage, out of casing

½ cup chopped onion

½ cup chopped celery

2 cups fine bread crumbs

2 ounces tomato paste

2-3 cups chicken broth

Chopped parsley

Olive oil

Salt and pepper

PROCEDURE

To prepare the stuffing, sauté sausage with a tablespoon of olive oil for 3 minutes. Add onion and sauté for 3 minutes. Add celery and continue cooking for a couple of minutes. Add tomato paste, chicken broth, and parsley and simmer for 2 minutes. Add bread crumbs, salt, and pepper. Remove from heat and stir until you achieve a texture suitable for stuffing.

To stuff and cook the goose, let the stuffing cool. Stuff the goose and close the opening with a couple of toothpicks or clamps. Place the goose on a rack in a shallow pan. Add the vegetables and wine, keeping the goose elevated above the liquids.

Cover the breast of the goose with bacon. Roast the goose at 400 degrees for about 2 ½ hours or until the internal temperature at the leg joint is 160 degrees. Baste frequently during the roasting process. When your goose is cooked, let it rest for half an hour. Remove and discard the bacon. If you wish to make a sauce, skim the fat and remove the vegetables. Add some chicken broth and reduce. Thicken if you wish with flour or cornstarch or arrowroot. Carve the goose, display on a platter, and spoon some sauce over it.

Rib Roast of Beef Roasted over Wood and Charcoal

This is a whole rib roast cooked on a covered BBQ fired by charcoal and wood. We prepare this occasionally at the Chef's Table with outstanding results.

Ingredients – For 15 Guests or More

1 whole boneless rib eye weighing about 10 to 12 pounds

10 garlic cloves, roughly chopped

¾ cup dry rub consisting of salt, pepper, dried sage, and dried rosemary; equal amounts of sage and rosemary, combined with salt and pepper to taste and ground together in a spice grinder

Procedure

Fire up a covered BBQ or Weber grill large enough to hold the rib roast on the side of the fire. Carefully remove the fat cap on top of the rib roast, keeping the fat cap whole if possible. Rub the herb/spice mixture generously on top of the meat. Distribute the garlic on top of the meat. Put back the fat cap, covering the seasonings. Tie the fat around the meat with string. Place the roast on the side of a hot fire (400 degrees) in your BBQ. Close the lid and let the meat roast for 45 minutes, after which you should check the roast and the heat levels. Now rotate the meat so that the side facing the fire is turned away from it. Add more coals or wood if necessary to keep a steady heat level. Our experience is that the roast will require 2 ½ to 3 hours of cooking. Look at it every half hour or so, turning it around. When it is done to your specifications (120 degrees for rare; 125 to 130 degrees for medium rare; 135 to 140 degrees for medium), take it off the grill, and let it stand for half an hour before carving and serving on a beautiful platter.

Roast Chicken

For roasting, I like to use the fattest chickens available– at least 6 pounds apiece – even heavier if I can find them.

Ingredients – For 8 Guests

1 fat roaster, at least 6 pounds

Seasonings ground together in a spice grinder:

1 tablespoon fennel seeds

½ teaspoon black pepper

¼ teaspoon salt

½ teaspoon paprika

Olive oil

3 garlic cloves, slivered

Juice from 3 lemons

1 whole lemon cut into quarters

6 cloves whole garlic

1 sweet onion cut into quarters

2 pounds aromatic vegetables to roast with the chicken: onions, leeks, carrots, other roots, garlic, shallots, scallions, your choice, any combination

3 cups dry white wine

Procedure

Heat the oven to 450 degrees. Wash the bird inside and out. Stuff the cavity with 1 whole lemon (cut into quarters), 6 garlic cloves, and 1 sweet onion cut into quarters. Close the cavity with a couple of toothpicks. Season the chicken with seasonings from the spice grinder. Brush with olive oil. Insert slivered garlic under the skin wherever you can. Place chicken on a rack in a shallow roasting pan. Place the aromatic vegetables around the rack. Add the wine. Roast the bird for about an hour, basting frequently. The bird is done when the thermometer reads 160 degrees at the joint between the leg and thigh. Let the bird rest for 20 minutes.

If you wish to make a sauce, skim the fat, remove the vegetables, and reduce the liquid. Add chicken broth if you need it and thicken with flour, cornstarch, or arrowroot.

Carve the chicken, arrange on a platter, and serve.

Leg of Lamb, Café Capriccio Style, Roasted on the Covered BBQ

Overnight marinating is preferred.

Ingredients – For 8 to 12 Guests

1 leg of lamb, 8 pounds, bone out, butterflied

For 1½ cup Marinade (described below)

1+ cup olive oil	3 bay leaves
1/3 cup white wine vinegar	2 tablespoons rosemary
6 cloves garlic	Salt and pepper

Procedure

To prepare the marinade, combine all ingredients in a blender and blend until everything is integrated and the texture is somewhat thick.

Trim the fat and the coarse tissue on the outside of the lamb. Pound the interior of the leg with a meat bat to smooth it, but not to flatten it. The meat should be roughly the same thickness top to bottom. Marinate the meat for several hours; overnight is better.

Heat the BBQ with charcoal and/or wood to around 400 degrees. Place the lamb over the coals for about 5 minutes on each side, then set it to the side of the fire so that it cooks by indirect heat. Roast covered for 45 minutes, then check the temperature. For me, lamb is perfect cooked to 135 degrees. Let it rest, then slice, arrange on a platter, and serve.

Roast Tenderloin of Beef

Tenderloin is less challenging than many other roasts but it is always appropriate for special occasions – and it can be magnificent on your chef's table. Ask the butcher to trim and tie the filet. Note that the tail is quite thin while the head is fat and unevenly shaped. You might also ask the butcher to trim and tie the head and either remove the tail or fold it back upon itself and tie that as well. If you leave the tail alone it will be cooked to a crisp!

Ingredients – For 10 Guests

1 beef tenderloin (filet of beef), 5 to 6 pounds, well trimmed

1 cup melted butter

Salt and pepper.

Procedure

Heat the oven to 500 degrees. Brush the tenderloin with butter, and season with salt, and pepper. Roast 25 minutes, basting with butter 2 or 3 times. Check the temperature after 25 minutes. For me, the ideal temperature is 125 degrees.

Let the beef rest for 15 minutes, then carve it and serve.

Roast Turkey with Seasoned Bread Stuffing

Turkey is the all purpose go-to big bird for many festive occasions. For this recipe, we will be stuffing a 20-pound turkey. For the stuffing, avoid hard, finely ground breadcrumbs; use soft bread instead. And a word of caution: turkeys are not easy to cook correctly. Overcooked turkey is a tough penance and undercooked turkey a nightmare. Cooking a turkey properly requires use of a meat thermometer no matter how skilled the master of the oven. If you can get a fresh bird from a local farm, buy it. Otherwise don't agonize over the quality of frozen turkeys found in supermarkets; they're usually fine. When using a frozen bird, defrost it beforehand overnight in the refrigerator.

Ingredients – For 15 or more Guests

1 turkey, 20 pounds

2 pounds rough-cut aromatic vegetables and herbs: onions, leeks, carrots, shallots, thyme, sage, garlic– your choice

Neck and giblets for broth

3 cups white wine

Bay leaves

Salt and pepper

For the Bread Stuffing:

10-12 cups of soft bread roughly cut from Italian or French

1 pound butter

2 cups chopped sweet onion

or scallion

1 cup chopped parsley

2 tablespoons dried sage

Salt and pepper

Procedures

Make a broth with the turkey neck together with giblets, onion, carrot, bay leaf, salt, and pepper. Cover with water and simmer for 1 hour to make the broth.

To prepare the stuffing, sauté onion in butter for 5 minutes. Add breadcrumbs, sage, parsley, and more butter as needed. Mix to blend and create a light stuffing that's not soggy.

If preparing a frozen turkey, defrost the turkey overnight in the refrigerator. Wash the thawed turkey thoroughly. Stuff the cavity without packing it too tight. Seal the cavity with clamps or skewers. Tie the tips of the legs together with string. Place the rough-cut vegetables in a roasting pan large enough to accommodate the turkey and the vegetables. Add 3 cups of white wine plus 1 cup of water. Place the stuffed turkey on a rack above the vegetables and liquid.

Heat the oven to 400 degrees. Roast the turkey, breast side down, for 45 minutes. After 45 minutes, turn the turkey on its side, baste, and roast for 45 minutes more. Turn the turkey on its other side and roast for another 45 minutes. Turn the turkey on its back and roast with the breast up for about 1 hour, basting frequently. (So far the turkey has cooked for 3 hours.) Test for doneness by inserting a thermometer into the thigh but not touching the bone, which is a heat conductor and will be hotter than the meat around it. When the turkey is cooked, let it rest for at least 20 minutes. The temperature will increase as the turkey rests. The correct temperature for turkey is 160 degrees.

To make a sauce or gravy, skim the fat from the roasting pan and remove the vegetables. Add some of the broth and reduce the liquid to achieve the desired taste. Adjust seasonings. Thicken with cornstarch, flour, or arrowroot. Carve the turkey when ready, display on a platter, and serve with sauce.

FRANCO

Franco Rua is now our leader, being the primary director of activities in both of our restaurants: Café Capriccio and Capriccio Saratoga.

Franco grew up playing with me in the kitchen at Café Capriccio, but not working seriously until he was in college at the local university, SUNY Albany. He worked in the kitchen a reasonable amount of time during his college years, but I did not press him believing his life as a kid and his academic work were top priority.

I always advised my children that restaurant life was a difficult choice and probably should be avoided, except under exceptional circumstances. Franco listened, but in the end he surprised me one day when the two of us were vacationing together in a town named Siderno, Calabria, on the Ionian Sea.

He was about to begin his last semester. We had just returned from a visit to the Archeological Museum in Reggio, Calabria, where are located the finest bronze figures from ancient Greece that exist in the world. These are known as the *Bronzi di Riace,* two bronze heroic figures discovered in 1972 off the coast of the Ionian seaside town of Riace, about 120 kilometers from Reggio, the capital city of the province of Calabria.

Franco and I were discussing archeology and his plans for graduate school on the beach when he told me that he had decided to join me at Café Capriccio instead of going on to graduate school. Part of the appeal for him was Café Capriccio's ongoing travel programs where we escort groups to Italy one or more times a year for cultural and culinary holidays. Franco had accompanied me on many of these excursions. Another appeal surely was his keen interest in food. And then he admitted that he had had enough of school for a while.

When I recovered from the shock of Franco's decision I told him to finish his degree and then come to work with me. First you will be my assistant, I said. Then we will begin to change roles; no one will notice.

Franco's developing stewardship of Café Capriccio is still in its formative years. But he is a quiet revolutionary making changes that few restaurant practitioners would undertake; changes that require extraordinary vision, skills, and discipline to accomplish. His culinary values are reflected not only in his exceptional cooking skills but, more to the revolutionary point, in his commitment to produce the "raw materials" for Café Capriccio's cuisine, and his willingness to do the work necessary to implement the vision.

Capriccio uses plenty of foods packaged for convenience; none is more important than San Marzano tomatoes, for example, or packaged baby lettuces. But, under Franco's leadership we have begun to take responsibility for self sufficiency and the quality of food we serve. These values are a throwback to my grandparents' immigrant experience.

Jeanette Stanziano, who has given me many ideas for this book, reminded me of an illuminating interview that we had read in the Magazine *La Cucina Italiana (May 2010)* with the Italian designer Massimo Vignelli. Vignelli speaks eloquently about a philosophy of food and cooking that Franco and I share and is central to the direction of Café Capriccio and Capriccio Saratoga under Franco's leadership. Moreover, Vignelli's comments seem to spring from the experience I described in the chapter about my family's table and reflect the lessons I learned from my grandparents. Vignelli says:

"(W)hat makes Italian food good is the raw material. It is the building block for the cuisine's identity. The Italians know how to foster the cultivation of excellent ingredients. I think the best thing for American food is a new focus on the quality of available ingredients. It's very difficult to cook without good, fresh materials. There's a lot to be learned from Italy's Slow Food movement."

This year, as in past years, Franco has planted two gardens to supply Café Capriccio and the Chef's Table. One at his grandmother's nearby home and one behind the Café Capriccio. He will have more than six varieties of tomatoes (seventy-five plants) that will produce a great bounty for Café Capriccio diners. We hope to preserve some tomatoes, as my mother and grandmother did fifty years ago. These gardens also contain most of the herbs we will use until the first frost, so we have probably a six months supply. We are also growing the usual vegetable varieties that are grown in the northeast

United States. We bake bread every day. Franco makes the sausages we serve at Café Capriccio, and we regularly produce fresh mozzarella for our delicious Caprese salad and our new Neapolitan pizza offerings.

One of this year's most exciting projects has been Franco's singular effort to create a slumeria within the walls of Café Capriccio. Franco's intention is to produce all of the exquisite cured meats that are associated with Italian cuisine. The results have been outstanding, and our family and friends have been enjoying Franco's sopressata, finocchiona, chorizo, guanciale, pancetta di maiale and pancetta di chinghiale, coppa, and most recently his pink and pungent prosciutto—all of which had been hanging in a special place for more than a year. At the appointed time we approached the hanging prosciutto with reverence, carefully sliced it, examined its color and texture, then tasted it with sacramental respect. Aaaahaa, *delizioso*. Another step back, it was, to the values we cherish. It was also a big step forward as we pursue those values now in the twenty-first century.

Like Massimo Vignelli, and my parents and grandparents, Franco is not "very interested in complicated cuisine or cooking; it disguises the ingredient, losing its inherent structure. I like tomatoes, not a foam made from tomatoes. If you have a superb tomato you don't need to mess with it—just eat it."

Not so many years ago I was disappointed to see a case of manufactured tomatoes delivered by a food purveyor to Café Capriccio in August, when good local tomatoes were widely available. I sent those tomatoes back and demanded that never again should we buy such a product at such a time. Now, with Franco in charge I can be sure that Café Capriccio's cooking and ingredients will reflect the now- revolutionary ideals of my parents and grandparents that inspired me and have been elevated to a new level by Franco Rua, the quiet revolutionary.

Sauté It

Sautéeing is much like braising, since foods are first browned in a pan and then cooked, usually on top of the stove, with liquids. Sometimes sautéed foods are cooked covered and sometimes uncovered. Sautéed foods typically cook faster than foods that require braising. A sauté pan should have a long handle to facilitate moving food around and also to provide some distance between the pan and your hand in order to avoid splattering oils and fats, which can plague the cook at the beginning of the sauté process. The sauté pans I prefer are of the nonstick, anodized varieties, like the Calphalon brand. These have the advantage of a slippery surface and durable construction, and they don't cause chemical reactions with acidic food. When I opened Café Capriccio thirty years ago a friend gave me three small sauté pans made by Calphalon. These have long handles and black surfaces. We use these pans in the restaurant every day to serve ravioli at the table. They remain in perfect condition, a quite remarkable fact.

The foods we sauté – fish fillets and veal scaloppini, for example – tend to be more delicate than those we braise. Some take only a few minutes. Many begin with a light flour dusting and are then browned in butter, olive oil, or a combination of the two. Virtually all the tender cuts of meat, and countless fish varieties, can be sautéed.

When cooking for large numbers of guests, a cook may have to use two sauté pans, which can make for an acrobatic exercise, or sauté in batches, keeping already cooked foods warm in the oven before plating. There is an endless variety of attractive and delicious sautéed dishes that can be prepared with infinite combinations of herbs, spices, vegetables, wines, and broths.

Below are some of our favorite sautéed dishes at Café Capriccio's Chef's Table that can become part of your personal-table repertory.

Steak Pizzaiola — Steak in the Style of the Pizza Maker

4 sirloin strip steaks,
about 1 inch thick apiece

1 can San Marzano tomatoes
(28 ounces), drained of juices

2 tablespoons olive oil

4 cloves garlic, chopped

¼ teaspoon hot pepper flakes

½ teaspoon dried oregano

Chopped parsley

Salt and pepper

Procedure

Season the steaks with salt, pepper, and oregano. Brown the steaks in a skillet for 2 minutes on each side. Remove the steaks from the skillet. Add olive oil and garlic, sauté for a minute. Don't burn the garlic. Add tomatoes, herbs, and spices. Simmer for 2 minutes. Add the steaks, cook with the tomato sauce for about 5 to 7 minutes for medium rare. Slice each steak into 6 slices. Arrange on a platter with sauce on top. Garnish with parsley and serve.

Tuna Steak Pizzaiola

Ingredients – 8 servings

4 tuna steaks weighing
about 6 oz. each

1 can San Marzano tomatoes
(28 ounces), drained of juices

2 tablespoons olive oil

4 cloves garlic, chopped

1 small can anchovies

½ cup pitted Calamata olives

2 tablespoons capers

¼ teaspoon hot pepper flakes

½ teaspoon dried oregano

Chopped parsley

Procedure

Season the tuna steaks with oregano and brush them with olive oil. Brown the steaks in a skillet for 2 minutes on each side. Remove the steaks from the skillet.

Add anchovies and garlic; sauté for a minute. Don't burn the garlic.

Add tomatoes, olives, capers, herbs, and spices. Simmer for several minutes.

Add the tuna steaks, cook with the tomato sauce for about 4 minutes for medium rare. Slice each tuna steak into 2 slices. Arrange on a platter with sauce on top. Garnish with parsley and serve.

Pepper Steak with Cognac

Ingredients – 8 Servings

4 sirloin strip loin steaks, each 1 inch thick

3 tablespoons crushed black peppercorns

Salt

3 tablespoons butter

1 tablespoon olive oil

½ cup of cognac or brandy

Procedure

Season the steaks with salt and peppercorns, pressing the spices into the steak on both sides. Allow the steak to stand at room temperature for at least 1 hour.

Heat a skillet. Add the butter and olive oil. Get it hot. Sear the steaks for 2 minutes on each side without turning it. Then turn it a couple of times, allowing about 8 minutes total cooking time for medium rare. After about 7 minutes, add the cognac. This will ignite, so be careful. The flames will quickly diminish. Swirl the steak around turning a couple of times to ensure that the brandy permeates the steak. When finished, slice the steak, arrange on a platter, pour the sauce over it, and serve.

Boneless Chicken Thighs with Marsala Wine

Ingredients – 8 servings

10 boneless chicken thighs
(1 plus for each guest)

3 ounces tomato paste

1 cup dry Marsala wine

2 cups chicken broth, or 2 cups water
with a teaspoon of chicken bouillon

4 tablespoons butter

4 tablespoons olive oil

3 cloves garlic

1 cup flour

Chopped parsley

Salt and pepper

Procedure

Remove the skin from the chicken thighs. Pound the thighs so that the meat is relatively even, increasing the width of each thigh by 10 to 15 percent. Season the meat with salt and pepper and fresh parsley. Dust the chicken with flour. Heat the skillet. Add the oil and butter and sauté the chicken for 2 minutes on each side, being sure to brown it. Remove the chicken and discard the fat.

Add 2 tablespoons olive oil, sauté the garlic for a minute, and then discard the garlic. Add the tomato paste and broth, stirring to create a smooth liquid. Return the chicken to the pan and add the Marsala. Let the chicken cook slowly, covered, for 15 minutes, turning a couple of times. When it is cooked, arrange the chicken on a platter, adjust the sauce. Spoon the sauce on top. Finish with parsley.

Veal Saltimbocca alla Romana

Scaloppine are thin slices of meat (veal in this case) weighing between 1 and 2 ounces. The best veal for this purpose is cut from the top round, but leg cuts are fine. Supermarkets usually offer thinly sliced veal from the leg that is recommended for scaloppine dishes. For this preparation, calculate 3 scaloppine for each diner. Assume that one pound of veal will yield 16 scaloppine.

Ingredients – 8 Servings

24 veal scaloppine

1 thin slice of prosciutto for each piece of veal

1 sage leaf for each piece of veal

3 cups white wine

1 stick butter

Flour

Olive oil

Toothpicks

Procedure

Use a mallet to flatten each scaloppina so that its width does not exceed 1/8 inch.

Attach 1 slice of prosciutto to each slice of veal. Place 1 fresh sage leaf on top of the prosciutto and secure both the prosciutto and sage leaf to the veal with a toothpick. Do not flour the veal. Use a sauté pan large enough to hold 8 scaloppine. Cover the bottom of the pan with butter and olive oil.

Saute the veal, prosciutto/sage side down, for about 1 minute. Turn and sauté the other side for an additional minute. Now add ¾ cup of wine and simmer for a couple of minutes. Transfer the veal to a warm platter and reserve the liquid. Repeat the process until all of the scaloppine are cooked. At the finish, add several tablespoons of butter to the pan and a couple of tablespoons of flour, along with 2 cups wine and the reserved liquids from previous batches. Scrape the pan and reduce the wine. Adjust for desired thickness. Return the veal to the pan for a minute. Finally, place the veal on a platter and spoon some the sauce over it. Serve immediately.

Chicken Breasts with Orange and Mint

Ingredients

Small chicken breast fillets,
1 per person

Chopped mint

Dry sherry

Olive oil

Butter

Chicken stock

Orange juice

Orange wedges

Orange zest

Salt and pepper

Procedure

Salt and pepper the chicken and sprinkle it with chopped mint. Dredge the chicken in flour. Heat the olive oil and butter together in a skillet and sauté the chicken to brown it on both sides. Add the sherry; calculate ½ cup for 4 small chicken breasts in a skillet. Let the sherry ignite – but be careful.

Add chicken broth and orange juice, equal proportions, for a total of 2 cups liquid per 4 breasts. Simmer uncovered for about 5 minutes. Remove the chicken from the skillet when it reaches 160 degrees. Reduce the sauce and adjust seasonings. Place the chicken on a platter, spoon sauce over it, garnish with orange wedges around, orange zest on top, and mint sprinkled throughout.

YONO

Yono Purnomo is the Capital Region's most decorated chef. Yono actually has a bit of blue blood in him, which has always shown in his elegant manner and impeccable dress. Born in Jakarta, Indonesia, he graduated from the culinary Academy Perhotelan Negara in his homeland, and received extraordinary training and experience in the splendid dining rooms aboard the SS Rotterdam, flagship of the Holland America Cruise Lines. After a fairy-tale shipboard romance, Yono married his beautiful and talented wife Donna, and the newlyweds settled in Albany, Donna's home town.

Yono and I began working together around 1977 in my first restaurant, Casa Verde, which I had just opened in 1976. Yono's training allowed him to know just about everything about food and hospitality by the time we met. In contrast, my inexperience was woeful. My first job in a restaurant was in my own restaurant. I possessed the unhappy combination of irrational exuberance together with a lack of relevant experience: As a restaurant owner, I was a threat to myself as well as to those around me.

Yono always tells our friends that I was his mentor, when the truth is that I knew little or nothing about restaurants in 1977, and he knew it all. Yono was MY Mentor, along with chef George Reece, a man for whom Yono and I have the highest respect and fond memories.

George Reece was an African American chef from Philadelphia about ten years my senior. He was working at an Asian restaurant in Albany when the place closed shortly after I had opened Casa Verde. He came to me for a job saying that he knew Italian cuisine, and, he said, "I can cook your style." It seems that George had worked for years with a knowledgeable Italian chef in Cleveland, Ohio. I hired him and soon discovered that he was indeed a master. George, Yono, and I worked together at Casa Verde and then, beginning in 1981, for three years at the Tanglewood Music Festival in Lenox, Massachusetts. Whenever George and I were in the kitchen together, which was often, he was my leader. George Reece was a brilliant chef, a wonderful guy, and the best cooking teacher I ever had. Some time before I opened Café Capriccio, George moved away from Albany and I lost contact with him. Recently I learned that he passed away from complications related to diabetes. This small tribute is trivial compared to George's contribution to my development. But I want the record to be clear that this man left his personal and professional mark on Yono and me. We often reminisce about our work together, including many highlights and wonderful memories.

I opened Casa Verde in October, 1976, and closed it on New Year's Eve, 1980, to pursue other follies. The following summer, Yono, George Reece, and I joined together again to be the official caterers at the Tanglewood Music Festival. This was in 1981. The Tanglewood experience involved operating a supper club for patrons before Boston Symphony concerts on Friday and Saturday evenings. It also involved special catered events such as cast parties and receptions for various events and occasions.

The supper club was located in a mansion named Seranak, the summer home of Serge Koussevitsky and his wife Natalie. Koussivitsky was the conductor of the Boston Symphony from 1924 to 1949, the period that also included the founding of Tanglewood in 1937. Seranak is an enormous mansion across the street from the Music Shed at Tanglewood, located on a hill overlooking a lake (the Stockbridge Bowl) and the beautiful Berkshire mountains.

Perhaps the most memorable event Yono and I organized together at Tanglewood occurred at the Tanglewood debut of John Williams, famous composer of music for films. He had recently been appointed conductor of the Boston Pops Orchestra. Everyone wanted to do something special for Maestro Williams, and Yono had the right idea. He gathered many of his Indonesian friends and some family, dressed them and himself all fabulously, and prepared the most unusual and interesting feast any of us had ever seen: a Rijsttafel, said to be the "crown jewel " of Indonesian cuisine.

The Rijsttaffel, indigenous to Indonesia, is a complex mix of culinary influences from Spain, Portugal, China, Holland, India, Britain, and other places. The Rijsttaffel includes many small dishes called *Sambals*. Meat and potato patties, yellow rice, vegetables with peanut sauce, barbecued seafood, banana fritters, grilled chicken with spicy sauces, various vegetable condiments, curried lentils, and cucumber bean salad were just some of the delectations.

On that memorable evening, the austere New England elegance of the Koussevitsky dining room at Seranak looked like the grand ballroom of the SS Rotterdam. Nobody could have brought that off except Yono. And did he himself look splendid, dressed in the regal splendor of his father's wedding attire.

Yono and I enjoyed many successes together, but we had one wild night at Café Capriccio which, I have to confess, was an ignominious moment in culinary history. I repeat it here as an act of contrition, in the interest of truth, complete disclosure, and abject humility.

I used to give cooking classes at Café Capriccio, sometimes accompanied by chefs who were friends of mine. I invited Yono to join me on September 8, 1997, for a cooking class entitled "The Indonesian/Italian Connections." I described it to potential guests in a news letter:

> "O baby. Yono and I have decided to create a new fusion cuisine (Indonesian/Italian) for the Monday Evening Gathering of Gentlemen-program at Café Capriccio. Although there are probably a sizeable number of Indonesian people in Italy, and some Italians in Indonesia, the world has not yet enjoyed the potential synthesis of these two great cuisines – UNTIL NOW! Yono and I have been collaborating for a couple of decades, so we are not strangers to each other's cooking styles, but we have never before attempted the ensuing culinary gymnastic exercises. Each course will be a little bit Italian and a little bit Indonesian. Are we embarking upon an important occasion in the gustatory history of the world? Worthy gentlemen with the courage to assemble with us on this evening will be the judge."

Yono's contributions that evening were perfectly executed and a credit to his culinary mastery: curried rack of lamb, for example, and a delicious South Pacific filling of exquisite delight for a canoli shell served for dessert. I, on the other hand, proposed an idea for the pasta course that I now regret but will nevertheless share, however shamelessly, with readers of this book:

Penne Mezzanina with Peanut Sauce

The pasta is cooked in the usual manner. The sauce is made as follows:

Ingredients

1 cup peanut oil

1 pound peanuts

1 medium size onion dices

4 cloves chopped garlic

pinch of red pepper flakes

salam leaf, citroen leaf

3 ounces brown sugar

salt to taste

Procedure

Fry peanuts in hot oil until cooked. Sauté onion, garlic, and red pepper.

Blend with 1 pint of water until smooth. Place blended ingredients into a pot and simmer while adding sugar, salam, and citroen. Cook until the sauce is smooth. Cook the pasta al dente, toss in the sauce and serve. *Delizioso!*"

YUCK. I'm sorry I did this to you, Yono. I ruined a perfectly good peanut sauce and embarrassed both of us. I wish to thank Yono here and now for never reminding me of this fiasco and for allowing the idea of Indonesian/Italian fusion cuisine to disappear like morning fog.

Yono's Curried Rack of Lamb

This is Yono's delicious recipe for curried rack of lamb. If you are feeding a crowd, you may need to prepare more than one.

Ingredients

Rack of Lamb

For the curry:

4 cloves garlic

Additional herbs and spices:
1 teaspoon sambal ulek (good luck),
2 teaspoons ground coriander,
1 teaspoon cumin, ½ teaspoon
tumeric, 3 cloves, ½ teaspoon
mustard seed, 3 bay leaves,

1 teaspoon black pepper

1 cup olive oil

1 ounce vinegar

1 cup seasoned
breadcrumbs

Procedure

Place herbs, spices, vinegar, and breadcrumbs into a blender, and slowly add oil until thick and smooth. Cover the rack of lamb with the marinade and marinate for 24 hours in a cool place. Roast the lamb in a hot oven 450 – 500 º F for about 30 to 40 minutes; internal temperature is about 130º F for medium rare. Let rest for 10 minutes, then cut into chops, and arrange on a platter garnished with greens.

Steam It

Steaming is so versatile, and comparatively easy, that this chapter will include a Christmas Eve feast of seven fishes, all prepared using a steamer. Because Asian cuisine includes many steamed foods, Asian markets often sell steamers in various sizes to meet your particular needs. None of them is expensive.

The steamer can be the cook's best friend when preparing feasts for the celebratory table. The steamer I use is simply a large pot of boiling water with a tight-fitting porous basket (mine is aluminum) and a secure lid. Bushels of vegetables and fish, among other foods, can be cooked in the steamer quickly, and with little fuss or mess. I suggest using the steamer for your chef's table feasts as a first stage in preparing an ingredient. Following stages could involve finishing it with a sauce, salsa, dressing, or marinade; combining it with other foods; or adding it to other foods to receive an appropriate finish.

There are a couple of general rules about steaming:

1. Be sure the basket is large enough to contain what you are steaming without overcrowding. This will ensure even cooking.
2. Use plenty of boiling water to create a powerful cooking medium.
3. Be attentive. Cooking with steam is a fast process.

Green Beans with Fried Peppers, Anchovies, Garlic, and Olive Oil

Ingredients

Fresh green beans, stems removed, cleaned; calculate 2 ounces per guest

Bell peppers: red, yellow and orange, proportionate to the quantity of green beans

Anchovies, as many as you like

Chopped garlic

Olive oil

Salt and pepper

Procedure

Prepare the steamer by boiling the water. Steam the green beans for 2 to 3 minutes, until they are finished to your desired taste – then plunge them into cold water to stop the cooking. Cut the peppers into strips and fry them in olive oil until they are caramelized, about 5 minutes. Add chopped garlic to the peppers about 1 minute before they are finished frying. Combine the peppers and green beans. Toss with olive oil, salt, and pepper, and finish with anchovies dispersed throughout. Arrange on a fancy platter. Serve warm or at room temperature.

Broccoli with Cherry Tomatoes and Hard Cooked Eggs

Ingredients

Fresh broccoli, trimmed to bite-sized pieces; calculate 2 ounces per person

Cherry tomatoes, cut lengthwise in half; several tomatoes per person

Hard boiled eggs; calculate about ¼

egg per person for the garnish

Olive oil

White vinegar

Salt and pepper

Procedure

Prepare the steamer by boiling the water. In another pot, boil eggs for about 10 minutes. Let the eggs cool, peel off the shell, and then slice into strips or quarters. Steam the broccoli for about 3 minutes. It should remain crisp and bright. Plunge the broccoli into ice water after cooking, then drain it and let it dry. When the broccoli is cool and dry, place it into a bowl. Add the cherry tomatoes to the broccoli. Season with salt and pepper, then toss with olive oil and vinegar (3 parts olive oil to 1 part vinegar). Arrange the broccoli and tomatoes on a platter and garnish with hard cooked eggs. Can be chilled or served at room temperature.

Asparagus with Tomato Salsa

Ingredients

Fresh asparagus, fibrous ends cut away; calculate 5 asparagus shoots per person

For the salsa:

Firm tomatoes, diced to fill 1 ½ cup; fresh are best

1 Celery heart with leaves, diced

Cilantro

Small sweet onion, diced

1 sweet pepper, any color, diced

4 tablespoons olive oil

Lime juice from 2 limes

Salt and pepper

Procedure

Prepare the steamer by boiling the water. Steam the asparagus for 2 minutes. Plunge into ice water to stop the cooking.

To make 2 cups of salsa, dice firm tomatoes to fill 1 ½ cup. You can buy canned diced tomatoes that will work for this purpose, although good fresh tomatoes are always best if you can find them. Combine celery, onion, and sweet bell pepper. Whisk together 4 tablespoons olive oil with the juice of 2 limes. Add cilantro, salt, and pepper to the mix. Toss everything together. Let the salsa rest in the refrigerator for an hour to integrate flavors.

Arrange the asparagus on a platter, then decorate with the salsa. I like the asparagus at room temperature and the salsa chilled.

Swiss Chard with Golden Beets

Ingredients

Fresh Swiss chard; calculate 2 ounces per person

Golden beets – red beets are fine if you cannot find golden

Olive oil

White vinegar

Salt and pepper

Procedure

Beets can be boiled, roasted, or steamed. They come in various sizes and can take time to cook. For this preparation I suggest that you boil them until they can be easily penetrated with a probe; this will be at an internal temperature of about 200 degrees. After the beets are cooked, let them cool, peel away the skin, and then cut them into bite-sized pieces. Toss them with olive oil, vinegar, salt, and pepper (3 parts olive oil, 1 part vinegar). Set aside at room temperature.

Prepare the steamer by boiling the water. Chop and clean the Swiss chard, trimming the very bottom but including most of the stalks. Steam the chard until the stalks are tender, about 5 minutes. Turn the chard onto a platter or into a bowl. Let it cool for a while, then toss with olive oil and vinegar. Add the beets, toss together, and serve. This dish is best at room temperature.

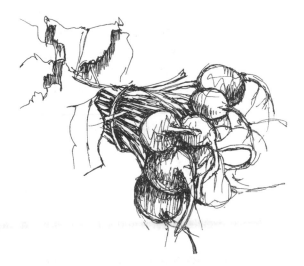

Rapini (Broccoli Raab) with White Beans

Rapini is a member of the turnip family, with broccoli-like flowers. It is one of the bitter greens Italians love and is a perfect partner with Tuscan-style white beans. Canned beans can be used or you can cook dried beans such as cannellini or great northern. Preparation time increases if using dried beans.

Ingredients

Broccoli raab; a 1 pound head will be enough for 10 people prepared this way

White beans; calculate ¼ cup of cooked beans per person

Fennel seeds, ground in a spice grinder: 1/8 teaspoon per cup

of beans

Chopped garlic to taste

Olive oil

Grated Pecorino Romano cheese

Salt and pepper

Procedure

To cook dried beans: Cover a one-pound bag of dried white beans with water, about one inch higher than the beans. Bring the water to a boil, and then turn it off. Let the beans rest covered in the boiled water for an hour, then season the beans with bay leaf. If you like, add a tablespoon of bacon fat, or a piece of prosciutto; anything "porky" is good for this purpose.

After the beans have soaked for an hour, season with salt and simmer for about 1½ hours. When the cooking liquid is completely absorbed, the cooking process is complete. Watch the beans while they cook: if more liquid is needed, add some; if there is too much, discard it. It's that simple.

Prepare the steamer by boiling the water. Steam the broccoli raab until it is tender, about 5 minutes. When the broccoli raab is cool, turn it into a bowl with the cooked beans. Dress everything with olive oil, finely chopped garlic, salt, pepper, crushed fennel seeds, and Pecorino Romano cheese. This preparation is excellent warm and at room temperature.

Tuscan Kale (Cavolo Nero) Stuffed with Sausage

Cavolo Nero is available at the Honest Weight Food Co-op in Albany, one of my primary sources throughout the year for fresh produce. It comes from California and is also know as Dino Kale. This is a dark green leafy vegetable, rather flat, long and thin as compared to curly kale. This vegetable is ubiquitous in Tuscany, where it is found in many forms on menus in virtually all restaurants. One head of kale typically has 7 to 10 leafy stalks, 8 to 12 inches long. Any sausage you like will be fine in this recipe. A simple dressing of olive oil, white vinegar, basil, salt, and pepper will work well for this preparation.

Ingredients

Tuscan Kale; calculate 2 or 3 leafy stalks per person

Sausage, out of the casing; calculate 1 ounce of sausage for each leaf of kale

Olive oil

Sliced tomatoes

Toothpicks: not exactly an ingredient but something useful for this preparation

Procedure

Prepare the steamer by boiling the water. Clean the kale, trim the end, and separate the stalks. Steam the kale for about 1 minute to soften it.

When cool enough to handle, wrap each stalk around 1 ounce of loose sausage so that the result resembles a stuffed grape leaf. Secure the folded mixture with a toothpick. When you have prepared a sufficient number of bundles, steam them for about 7 minutes, until the sausage is cooked to 160 degrees internal temperature. After steaming, arrange on a platter, drizzle with olive oil, and garnish with sliced tomatoes.

La Vigilia di Natale: An Italian Christmas Eve Dinner with Seven Courses of Fish.

To prove how versatile is our powerful steam cooker, I am including recipes for 7 courses of fish traditionally eaten by families on Christmas Eve. The fish for each course will be steamed and then finished as shown in each recipe. Pomegranate is a dazzling red-colored fruit with a flavor that is both sweet and tart. Preparing it is a worthwhile effort.

Scallops with Mixed Greens and Pomegranate

Scallops should marinate an hour before being steamed.

Ingredients

Large scallops, 10 or fewer to the pound; calculate 2 scallops per person

Mesclun greens, with as large a variety of baby lettuces as you can find;

½ cup of lettuce per person

Pomegranate—1 or 2

Dressing: olive oil, white vinegar, basil, salt, and pepper

Procedure

To make the dressing, whisk together olive oil, vinegar, chopped basil, salt, and pepper (3 parts olive oil to 1 part vinegar, other ingredients to your taste).

Marinate the scallops in the dressing for 1 hour or longer; keep refrigerated.

Cut the pomegranate in half; remove the seeds and surrounding red pulp. Discard everything else. Set aside.

Place the mesclun greens into a bowl.

Steam the scallops until they are cooked to your taste; 3 to 5 minutes should be enough time. Allow the scallops to cool, then toss them in the marinade. Dress the greens with the same marinade.

Arrange the scallops on a platter around the greens and garnish with the brilliant red pomegranate.

Calamari with Potatoes and Olive/Pepper Tapenade

You can buy roasted red peppers in cans and jars that work well for this purpose. You will need about 8 ounces. If you roast your own peppers, burn the skin off by placing them over a fire on your gas stove. Turn them to blacken evenly. When they are mostly black, remove them from the fire, let them cool, then run the peppers under cold water. Peel the skin and remove the core: presto, "roasted" peppers.

Ingredients

Roasted red peppers, about 8 ounces

Calamari, cleaned; calculate 2 ounces for each guest

Red skin potatoes, cut into half-inch cubes; calculate a couple of tablespoons for each 2 ounces serving of calamari

Lemon wedges

For 1½ cups of olive tapenade:

½ cup Calamata olives, pitted

2 bell peppers, red, roasted, skin peeled

Anchovies, one small can will do

2 tablespoons capers

2 cloves garlic

Procedure

To prepare the tapenade, combine olives, peppers, and the other tapenade ingredients in a blender. Blend the ingredients to leave some texture; do not puree.

Prepare the steamer by boiling water. Steam the diced potatoes until they are tender. Place into a bowl.

Cut the calamari into rings ¼ inch thick. Steam the calamari for about 5 to 7 minutes depending on its thickness. Combine the calamari and the potatoes; let them cool for a few minutes.

Add the tapenade and toss, integrating the tapenade, potatoes and calamari. Arrange on a platter and garnish with lemon wedges. Good warm and at room temperature.

Smelts with *Radicchio Rosso*, Radishes and Tomatoes, Salsa Verde

Smelts are small fish that migrate from their salt water habitats to spawn in fresh water. We buy them flash frozen, cleaned, and headless. Traditionally, smelts are deep fried, but I have found that steaming is an excellent way to prepare them. After steaming, smelts are firm and can be dressed in many interesting ways.

Ingredients

Smelts, cleaned, heads off; calculate 3 per person

Fresh radishes, sliced thin, as many as you like

Radicchio rosso, 1 head of radicchio for every 4 persons at the table

Tomatoes, proportionate quantity based on tomato size and your discretion

FOR THE SALSA VERDE:

1 bunch flat parsley, trimmed

½ cup basil

2 tablespoons capers

4 anchovies

1 clove garlic

Juice from 2 lemons

½ cup olive oil

2 tablespoons white vinegar

Salt and pepper

Procedure

To prepare the salsa, combine all salsa ingredients in a blender and process slowly to create some texture; do not puree.

Chop the radicchio as you wish and place into a bowl. Add the sliced radishes. Cut the tomatoes and add to the salad. Grape tomatoes cut in half work well, as do other varieties.

Prepare the steamer by boiling water. Steam the smelts for about 2 minutes. Let them cool. Toss the red salad with the salsa verde.

Arrange the smelts in and around the salad and dress them with salsa verde. Garnish with lemon wedges.

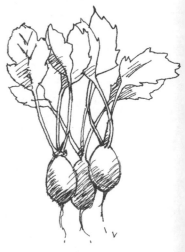

Snap Peas with Shrimp

Shrimp should be in the 15 to 21 per pound range. They can be fresh or frozen. If frozen, they can be cooked frozen. The tremendous heat of the steamer will allow you to cook frozen shrimp in a few minutes.

Ingredients

Fresh snap peas; calculate a couple of ounces per person

Sizeable shrimp; calculate 2 or 3 shrimp per person; peeled and cleaned

Diced red peppers, uncooked, enough to infuse the dish with color and crisp texture

Vinaigrette to dress the salad: olive oil, Dijon mustard, lemon juice, parsley, salt, and pepper

Procedure

To make the dressing, use 3 parts olive oil to 1 part lemon juice, adding mustard, herbs, and spices to taste.

Prepare the steamer by boiling the water. Pluck the snap pea stems and pull off the fibrous strings. Steam the snap peas for 1 ½ minutes. They should remain crisp. Plunge them into cold water after steaming. Drain them and let them dry. Clean and peel the shrimp if necessary. (You can buy them cleaned and ready to cook.) Steam the shrimp until they are cooked through. Allow the shrimp to cool. Combine the shrimp and snap peas together with diced red pepper. Dress with vinaigrette, toss, and arrange on a platter. Best served chilled.

Baccala with Aioli, Tomatoes, and Olives over Crostini

Baccala is dried salt cod whose preservation technique was developed by Portuguese sailors in the 16th century. The process involves salting and drying fresh cod, thus to preserve it. To refresh the cod, cooks have to soak it in several changes of water for about 24 hours. Baccala can be found in many supermarkets and specialty stores.

Ingredients

Salt cod; calculate 2 ounces per diner

per person

Cold tap water for soaking— for 24 hours

Pitted olives, chopped; calculate 1 teaspoon per diner

Plum tomatoes sliced in quarters, lengthwise; calculate ½ tomato

Long loaf of crusty bread

For 1 cup of Aioli (garlic mayonnaise):

1 cup olive oil

1 slice white bread soaked in water and squeezed dry

4 garlic cloves

2 tablespoons lemon juice

Chopped parsley

2 egg yolks

Pinch of salt

Procedure

For the baccala, cut the salt cod into 1 inch cubes and soak in several changes of water for 24 hours.

To prepare the aioli, combine garlic, bread, egg yolks, lemon juice, and salt in a food processor. Turn on the food processor and gradually add the oil until the mixture is thick.

Prepare the crostini by toasting small rounds of crusty bread in the oven. Calculate 2 rounds per person.

Prepare the steamer by boiling water. Steam the baccala for about 5 minutes. Remove, break up the fish, and place into a bowl. Steam the tomatoes for about 1 minute. Combine the baccala and olives. Toss with a light covering of aioli. Arrange on crostini with a wedge of tomato. Finish with chopped parsley.

Filet of Salmon with Lemon and Herbs

Ingredients

Salmon filets cut into 3 ounce servings

Lemon juice; calculate 1 tablespoon for each piece of salmon

Chopped parsley

Chopped thyme

Lemon wedges

Lemon zest

Procedure

Prepare the steamer by boiling the water. Steam the salmon for about 4 minutes; it should be pink and juicy inside. Arrange cooked salmon pieces on a platter with mixed greens underneath. Garnish with lemon juice, lemon zest, fresh herbs, and lemon wedges all around. This can be served warm or at room temperature.

Timpano

It is fitting to conclude this history of Café Capriccio's Chef's Table with a recollection of how it began on a memorable April Fool's day three years before the millennium. I had just completed the renovations that created the Chef's Table, which I then thought to name the Cooking and Wine School. As a grand inaugural I decided to offer a cooking program featuring *Timpano di Maccheroni.* from the then-popular film *The Big Night.*

The Big Night is a story about two brothers recently emigrated from Italy struggling to operate an "authentic" Italian restaurant in a small New Jersey town – a town whose residents prefer the style of cooking now featured in the chain restaurants that dominate America. The plot revolves around preparation of a grand feast for a special occasion, including a marvelous dish called *timpano di maccheroni.* Although the feast consists of many glorious courses, viewers seem only to be impressed by the *timpano,* a preparation that continues to fascinate people fifteen years after the film was introduced.

The term *timpano* is a dialect variation of a classic preparation called *timballo.* The Italian word is related to "kettledrum" in translation, and the preparation featured in the movie is fundamentally a casserole wrapped in pastry dough, shaped like a drum. We have been serving this dish the Chef's Table for lo these many years. We normally include it as one of our antipasti, although it is sufficiently abundant to constitute a robust meal, well suited to satisfy the hunger and nutritional needs of, say, a cross-country ski team after a tough competition. It will make a fabulous contribution to your chef's table feast on a very special occasion. It is also a big project. Do not be reluctant to seek help slicing, dicing, mixing, and cooking the many ingredients.

Italians prepare *timballi* in many ways, filling the drum with everything from little birds (*uccellini*) to candied fruits. Ours will follow the lines of the movie, although details of the preparation were not revealed in the film, only the majestic presentation.

Our technique is this:

> Line a 10-inch spring-form pan, bottom and sides, with pastry dough.
>
> Fill it, in layers, with a rich variety of meats, vegetables, pasta, cheese, hard-boiled eggs, and seasonings. After the ingredients are assembled, cover the top with more pastry dough and coat the top with egg-wash.
>
> Bake at 400 degrees for about 45 minutes, until the top is deeply colored and crisp. Let it stand for 30 minutes, then open up the spring-form, releasing the pastry dome. Cut the *timpano* into wedges and serve.

Timpano

This will easily serve 12 guests.

Utensils

1 spring-form baking pan, 10"

Pastry dough

Do yourself a favor by using commercial puff pastry found in the freezer section of supermarkets. There are enough other steps in this preparation to satisfy your cooking interests without the demanding dough-making part. You will need 2 packages that weigh 12 ounces each. Thaw them in the refrigerator the night before preparing this dish. When ready to line the spring-form, roll the dough to increase its volume by about thirty percent (and reduce its thickness correspondingly), and line the pan.

Polpettone (meatballs)

We will make one giant meatball in the shape of a meatloaf which will be sliced into the pastry drum.

Ingredients

1 pound ground beef, pork, veal, chicken – your choice, any combination

½ cup bread crumbs

2 eggs

4 garlic cloves, minced

5 tablespoons chopped parsley

½ cup Pecorino Romano, grated

Salt and pepper

Mix all ingredients, shape into a meatloaf, bake at 400 degrees for 30 minutes.

Sausage

Use at least 2 kinds of sausage: pork, chicken, turkey, pheasant, rabbit, lamb, your choice. Bake the sausages until they are cooked through, about 20 minutes at 400 degrees.

Chicken

Use 2 boneless chicken breasts or thighs. Season the chicken with salt, pepper, fresh herbs such as rosemary or sage, and then brush with olive oil. Grill the bird on both sides. Total cooking time is 10 minutes.

Vegetables

1 medium eggplant	3 tablespoons olive oil
2 bell peppers	3 garlic cloves minced
1 zucchini	Fresh basil
2 cups San Marzano tomatoes, juices strained	Parsley, chopped

Slice the eggplant ¼-inch thick. Cut the peppers on both ends, take out the core and flatten the sides for grilling. Cut the zucchini in half lengthwise. Brush the vegetables with olive oil, sprinkle with salt and pepper, and then grill for a few minutes on each side. Crush the tomatoes, add the olive oil, garlic, parsley, and basil.

Pasta

One pound *farfalle* (butterflies, also known as bow ties). Cook the pasta *al dente,* 6 or 7 minutes, drain it and immediately rinse with cold water to stop the cooking. Dress the pasta with the Italian plum tomatoes that have been crushed and seasoned, as described above.

Cheese

Use ½ cup grated mozzarella and ½ cup of grated Pecorino Romano.

Hard Boiled Eggs

Boil 6 eggs for 10 minutes, let them cool, then remove the shells.

To Assemble the *Timpano*

All ingredients described above should be cut for distribution within the pastry dome and organized for final assembly. Nothing should be hot.

Dust the thawed pastry dough with a little flour. Roll the dough to increase its volume by thirty percent. Butter the inside bottom and sides of a spring-form pan. Arrange a layer of dough on the bottom and sides of the spring-form. Arrange the ingredients in layers beginning with pasta. Use your imagination when creating the layered arrangement, considering color and contrasts of tastes and textures. Place the hard-boiled eggs so that they will be cut diagonally when the *timpano* is sliced. Cover the stuffed pastry dome with more puff pastry, sealing the edges. Brush with egg wash and bake at 400 degrees for about 45 minutes, until the top is deeply colored and crisp. Let stand for half an hour, then remove the sides of the spring-form and present the finished product at your table. Cut into generous wedges and serve.

INDEX

NOTES

NOTES

Notes

NOTES

About the Illustrator:

Elisabeth L. Vines has been illustrating as long as she could hold a pencil, but this is her first cookbook. Besides creating oil paintings based on photographs, she illustrates her life as an Associate Professor of Humanities at Albany College of Pharmacy and Health Sciences.